"Whoever says that humans can't fly hasn't read Barbara Wilder's book. While reading her book and taking the companion course, I discovered my wings. I glided back into the past, sailed through the present, and soared into the future. The journey was exhilarating, breathtaking, and mystical. Prepare to find your own wings, dust them off, and take flight."

— Ann Tinkham, instructional designer/writer

"Barbara Wilder's book, *Embracing Your Power Woman*, is a real treasure that will fill your hearts and souls with guidelines and experiences that will change your life. She teaches us what it means to embrace our own feminine power within and without, and pulls the reader into a spiritual sense of wellness."

— Christine Hibbard, Ph.D., psychotherapist and university professor

"Barbara Wilder has a knowing that transcends time and space. She takes you on a journey back to your own source. What a precious gift and a tremendously important work for the feminine. It has been a life-saving drink in the desert known as midlife. Barbara is a bright star, inspiring the 45+ generation."

— Kathleen Krentz, businesswoman

"Barbara Wilder has a wonderful gift for life and a great wisdom about the Spirit. Doing the *Embracing Your Power Woman* work, I began to see an opportunity for deeply enriched growth, a fertile time to celebrate who I am, and an awakening of long forgotten dreams. Being over 55 no longer feels like riding a stationary bicycle, but a positive dynamic journey that continues to amaze me."

— Connie Redak, florist

"Since doing *Embracing Your Power Woman*, I have had such ease in my personal relationships. New areas of my work are unfolding in the most effortless, wonderful way. I love this course. Barbara is a brilliant, compassionate writer and teacher who brings us back to the joy of being women."

— Bea Enright, yoga teacher

"Since doing *Embracing Your Power Woman*, I have become much more aware of my strength, my wisdom and my own magnificence. Using the tools and exercises from the course gives me something to hold on to whenever I get depressed. They put me back into a positive mood and a forward movement. I am beginning to trust that I am truly an artist, not just a mom and a breadwinner."

— Marilyn McVey, artist

"Barbara Wilder's *Embracing Your Power Woman* is empowering, enlightening and comforting. The work comes from her heart and her feminine energy in a way that satisfies what is missing in life. *Embracing Your Power Woman* will be a part of my library and my gift giving for special friends forever."

— Mary D. Midkiff, author, *She Flies Without Wings: How Horses Touch a Woman's Soul*

"Using her Eleven Points of Power that form the backbone for *Embracing Your Power Woman*, Barbara Wilder astutely directs women through passages in their lives to a final reckoning with their freedom and all the choices this entails. This wise journey is one that all women who want to lead a life well lived should wholeheartedly explore."

— Barbara Darling, public relations specialist and journalist

"In her compelling *Embracing Your Power Woman*, Barbara Wilder has provided a stunningly heartfelt and user-friendly roadmap to get us to our rightful place of power and meaning!"

— Lisa Trank, publicist, writer, and mother of three girls under 5

"*Embracing Your Power Woman* is a practical workbook that provides the inspiration and tools to excavate buried dreams and bring them to life in the second half of life. Every woman over 40 should read this book. I am buying a copy for all of my long lost and newfound girlfriends."

— Donna Druchunas, author of *The Knitted Rug* and *Arctic Lace*

"Participating in the *Embracing Your Power Woman* course has been an amazing journey. The material, games and exercises, and Barbara's wisdom and guidance allowed me to examine my innermost thoughts and feelings. Having the 'inner light bulbs' go on and finally understanding that we each have a place and purpose in the grand universe is such a wonderful gift."

— Vickie Terry, business consultant

"If nonviolence is the law of our being, the future is with women."

– Mahatma Gandhi

ALSO BY BARBARA WILDER

Money Is Love: Reconnecting to the Sacred Origins of Money

EMBRACING YOUR POWER WOMAN

11 Steps to Coming of Age in Mid-Life

BY

BARBARA WILDER

WILD OX PRESS

BOULDER, CO

Published by Wild Ox Press, June 5, 2005
ISBN 0-9673346-2-4
Second Printing, October 2005

This book was made possible by
The Ladder Foundation - Foxfire Studios
Boulder, Colorado

Author's Photographs by Jack Greene
Cover & Book Design by LLPrindle Design

Printed in the United States by United Graphics, Inc.

Wild Ox Press
P.O. Box 3304
Boulder, CO 80307-3304

For my sisters the world over
and for my mother, Clara Coulson,
who, eleven years after her death, has become
my beloved companion in this work

TABLE OF CONTENTS

ACKNOWLEDGEMENTS

I have so many people to thank for helping me with this book. It has been a long labor of love and my gratitude is deeply heartfelt. To begin I wish to acknowledge all the beautiful Power Women who worked with me in my workshops as I developed this course. Together we forged a new path through the wildness of midlife.

With all my heart, I thank Parker Johnson, a young man who had the vision and wisdom to understand that a healthy future cannot exist without women embracing their power. It was this wisdom that led him to invest his money and his loving intention to take this book to publication. And thanks also to another young man, Bruce Holsinger, a medieval scholar, who was so excited by this book that he volunteered his editorial skills in its early stages.

I gratefully acknowledge the enormously gifted Jennifer Heath, who worked on this project as my editor. Her talent has enhanced this work immensely. And thank you to Laurie Prindle for the rich artistry with which she designed the book and it's cover. Also, I am eternally grateful to Marilyn McGuire for her belief in this project and her willingness to lend her talent and love to getting it out into the world.

Many thanks to my life-long girlfriends: Hope Perello, Judy Simmons, Michele Warren, Elissa Kennedy, and my newer girlfriends Jennifer Heath, Anna Frost, and Nancy Foss, who have all been my sounding boards, my muses, my mirrors, and at times, my salvation.

Special thanks go to the women of my Crocker Elementary School Brownie troop: Buffy Ford Stewart, Diane Sue Heller, Bonnie Bonetti Bell, Ellen Makiney Flowers, Kathy Doughty, Carolyn Cucchi Vinson, Cindy Crowell Cotton, Marcia Rapp Brown, and Vicki DeSmet Blunt, with whom I reunited a couple of summers ago for the first time in forty-something years. They showed me the true beauty of women's friendships and our ability to leave behind our childhood wounds and find in our differences the seeds of our similarities.

Additionally, I thank Betty Pritchett, my amazing mother-in-law, who went back to college at fifty and inspired much of my first work about women at midlife. I thank her also for opening her heart and her family to me and for her constant support of my work and my dreams.

I also must thank my incredible team of enlightened teachers and healers who have been there for me through the incredible process of birthing this work: Jim Galbiati, Brian Ray, Marianne Weidlein, and Margaret Jacobs.

I thank, Patrick Prtichett, the husband who loved and nurtured me through my menopausal years. And finally, I thank my son, Sean Harrison, who has been my best friend, my teacher, and my guide in so many ways throughout our lives together.

FOREWORD

More of us are entering the second half of our lives than at any other time in history. Our numbers are growing rapidly, and as life expectancy continues to rise, more of us will find ourselves living much longer as elders than did our parents and grandparents.

These extra years, even decades, extend the blessing of life. Yet in many ways we are not prepared to live them fully. Our culture has lost the capacity to acknowledge and value elders the way many other cultures around the world do. We have forgotten the rites of passage that help us learn to become wise elders, actively participating in our communities and living a deep, fulfilling life. Unfortunately, our culture's current perspective is that the second half of life offers only decline, disease, despair, and death.

If we are to live our best second half of life, to embrace these years and flourish in them, we need to consciously shift our cultural perspective. It is time. We have only to look at the shocking fact that America has the world's highest suicide rate among elders to know that things must change. We can no longer ignore the wisdom that is irrevocably lost to future generations when our elders are marginalized or rendered invisible. The more challenging our world, the more we need our elders with us to share the lessons they have learned, to lend us their problem-solving skills, and to enhance our lives by imparting their unique gifts.

The rites of passage from birth to fifty years of age are well defined. We may go to school, get our first job, find life partners, raise a family, develop a career, and contribute to our communities. But the skills we developed during the first half of life are not adequate, nor are they appropriate, to support us in the second half; the tasks and requirements for growth and change are completely different. From age fifty onward, we know that there will be four broad frontiers to face:

- Retirement: from what, toward what?
- The possibility of becoming a mentor, a steward, or a grandparent.
- Coping with the natural challenges of maintaining the health of an aging body.
- Mortality: losing our loved ones, and the inevitability of our own death.

Each of these frontiers will demand from us very different attitudes, disciplines, and life skills, many of which have not yet been clearly associated with increased longevity. Each frontier will challenge us to be courageous in the face of our fears. This new terrain promises to be both daunting and exciting.

The second half of life is the ultimate initiation. In it, we encounter those new, unexpected, unfamiliar, and unknowable moments that remind us that we are a sacred mystery made manifest. If we truly understand what is required of us at this stage, we are blessed with an enormous opportunity to develop and embody wisdom and character. We enjoy limitless possibilities to restore, renew, and heal ourselves. And because of our increased longevity, for the first time in history we also have the opportunity to create a map of spiritual maturity for future generations to use as they enter their own later years.

The second half of life presents us with the opportunity to develop increased depth, integrity, and character—or not. The choice is always ours. Although the second half of life issues are not gender specific, they are deeply a part of all human development.

Embracing Your Power Woman by Barbara Wilder is an invaluable contribution to reclaiming and expressing the healthy feminine, which does not move into drama or collapse, nor eccentricity and rebellion. In the second half of life, the healthy feminine recognizes that this passage is a road of initiation, not a road of victimization or re-working past issues. The past is reviewed to cull the wisdom gained rather than indulging in old wounds or stories. Her book provides 11 steps that specifically empower women to claim fully who they are beyond family conditioning and cultural imprinting.

Angeles Arrien, Ph.D.
Author of *The Second Half of Life: Opening to the Eight Gates of Wisdom*

EMBRACING YOUR POWER WOMAN

Introduction

"I see the wise woman.
She carries a blanket of compassion.
She wears a robe of wisdom…
From her shoulder, a mantle of power flows."

– Susun Weed

When I fell into midlife somewhere in the beginning of my forties, I struggled alone to understand and accept what was happening to me. I began having hot flashes before the rest of my friends. My mother had mysteriously forgotten that she'd ever been through menopause, and there was a dearth of reference material on the subject. So I read what I could find, and used the tools and practices I had acquired in my years studying and teaching spiritual growth and healing to plow my way into the next phase of my life.

Once I had made some headway, I realized that what lay on the other side of menopause was the promise of an exciting and powerful new woman. I kept going, delving into the dark corners of my psyche to release the old me, and excavate the new. Sometimes I spent days and even weeks, depressed, obsessed by thoughts of death and dying. At other times I felt energized, and brand-new ideas would pop effortlessly into my mind. Yes, there were bouts of crying, hot flashes, and a general sense of loss, followed by days of frustration. But all the while, there was an underlying sense of excitement bubbling beneath the headaches and hot flashes.

At the time, I worked in Hollywood, struggling to produce films with female leads. But the projects loved by mid-life women like my producing partners and myself were the furthest thing from the criteria of the young male-oriented film industry in the early 1990s. Realizing that I needed to live in a more supportive environment for this crucial period of my life, and aided by a nudge from Mother Earth in the guise of the 1994 Northridge earthquake, I packed my bags, and, along with my husband, headed for a new place and a new life.

We landed in Boulder, Colorado, where I found clean air to breath, magnificent mountains to explore, and like-minded people. Except for the fact that we couldn't find work, the place was idyllic for this change in my life. As I hiked through Colorado's exquisite, rugged landscape I began to feel support from the environment, and each day, fresh insights made my life more and more fun to live. I was also faced with new challenges, both physical and financial, but as I faced them, and moved through them, I found I was building new muscles. These spiritual muscles would eventually become the infrastructure of my Power Woman.

After awhile, I realized that although things had seemed random and fate had seemed to jostle me blindly to this new phase in my life, I had, in fact, taken specific steps on an initiatory journey. Around me, I saw other women struggling with these same issues, and in 1998, I decided to share what I had learned so far by preparing and teaching a course on becoming a Power Woman. At that time, I was also leading groups through Julia Cameron's book, *The Artist's Way*, a journey to embracing one's creativity. Therefore, I wanted to give the women in my circle essays and exercises as I had done with the Artist's Way groups. In the planning stages of this book, I simply jotted down some of my thoughts and devised a few exercises each week to pass around at the end of class. Over time, working with circles of diverse women, revising and adding, this book was born.

What we discovered along the way was each of us was becoming a new kind of woman, a woman who had biologically completed the child-bearing years, whether still raising children or not, and yet who was not yet the wise-woman Crone we had expected to find on the other side of menopause. She was not Crone-like at all! She was still youthful, active, and ready for new challenges, and most importantly, she was ready to fulfill her life's true purpose.

Today, as I travel around the world leading my workshops, I find that many mid-life women are struggling with relationship problems, physical exhaustion, depression, money issues, and questioning of their own self-worth. Not surprising, since we have no guides to follow into and through this phase of our lives.

In times long past, in the era before written history, when women and the feminine energy were honored, there were sacred rituals and initiations held in a circle of women for the major life transitions. Scholars believe these rituals and initiations helped women channel and embrace the emotional and spiritual energies brought on by our biological changes. Without guidance, the biological transitions are often so confusing that they lead to anger, frustration, and even depression.

This book is a course that guides women through midlife and suggests eleven initiatory steps of power into, through, and beyond this transition. As we mid-life women are able to work in a sacred initiatory way to transition into this next phase, we will then be able to create rituals and initiations for younger women and girls coming up behind us and thus bring joy, excitement, and fulfillment to the other stages of feminine life, adolescence, and motherhood.

In my many years of working with women, I have come to believe that we of the baby-boomer generation (women born between 1946 and 1964) are in the process of developing a new stage of life, the Power Woman stage. It seems to me, all women have the potential to become Power Women as we emerge on the other side of menopause. This Power is not given. It is achieved. To become a Power Woman we must be proactive participants in the birth of our new selves. Luckily, the hormonal shift between our childbearing biology and our post-menopausal biology affects not only our bodies but also our brains, infusing them with a potent new spark of energy, intuition, and wisdom, igniting our imaginations and fueling our willingness to make the leap.

Our Power Woman has her genesis somewhere in our forties when a majority of us begin peri-menopause. As we reach menopause in our late forties to mid-fifties we are entrenched in this new phase of our lives, and by the time we have completed our menopausal journey, our Power Woman, if nurtured and supported, will be born.

In the ancient vision of womanhood, there were thought to be three stages of life: Maiden, Mother, and Crone. But as we live longer, healthier lives, the number of years between menopause and death are increasing, offering us an extra thirty or forty years of activity before we move into the wise-woman Crone stage, in what I believe will be in our late seventies or eighties or later.

As we emerge from our childbearing years, in which we were emotionally and biologically focused on our Yin energy, we begin to expand into our Yang energy. We begin to focus the feminine qualities we possess in a more dynamic and outgoing, or Yang, way. Men do the opposite. As men reach midlife, they move from Yang energy and begin expressing their masculine qualities in a more inward-focused, Yin way. That's why many men who never felt comfortable in roles around the home in their younger years find activities such as gardening, cooking, and playing with the

grandchildren so enjoyable in their later years. This is explained by our biological hormonal changes, as Joan Borysenko tells us in her book *A Woman's
Book of Life*. As women's estrogen levels become lower, our testosterone levels increase. This happens in the reverse in men, with their testosterone
lowering and their estrogen levels rising.

Women have a natural ability and desire to nurture, to take care of
others. But now, as we move into the next step in our lives, no matter how
we chose to live the first half of our lives, we are being urged to turn this
nurturing toward ourselves. And no matter how we lived during the years
before midlife—whether as stay-at-home moms, career women, or a combination of both—and no matter what our sexual orientation was and is,
we are all being called to become Power Women.

Our emerging Power Women need care, love, and training. We, ourselves,
in company with our peer sisters, are the best qualified for the job.

Society has never experienced the Power Women that we are becoming. Until now, society has held that post-menopausal women had no
worth. Even today after forty years of feminism, the media still glorify the
girl-woman. There is no traditional place for women in the second half of
life other than as sweet little grandmothers or vaguely wise old Crones. But
this generation of mid-life and midlife-plus women isn't going to accept
marginalization. We are powerful, potent, and ready for a change.

While I was preparing this book for publication I attended a conference in New York City on the weekend of September 11, 2004, sponsored
by Omega Institute and Eve Ensler's V-Day, called "Women and Power: Our
Time to Lead." The presenters and attendees at the conference were women
of all ages. It was exciting to witness so many women in the second half of
life sharing their knowledge, their life experience, and their abilities and
desire to take a powerful stance to make a difference. The energy at the conference—which was attended by more than 1200 women from all over the
country and the world—was emotionally, mentally, and spiritually impassioned. As I cheered, cried, and took assiduous notes with my 1200 sisters
over the course of the four-day event, I thought about how best I could
share this experience with my readers. I realized that women reading and
engaging in the work of *Embracing Your Power Woman* could experience this

level of excitement in their own homes and circles. As we prepared to leave the conference Elizabeth Lesser, co-founder of Omega Institute, and the "Weaver" introducing all the events and integrating all the strands of the conference, charged us to take the lessons and passion we had gleaned back to our homes, our communities, and to our women's groups and circles.

During a panel discussion with conference speakers, Jane Fonda spoke at length about her own emotional healing and growth over the past several years, noting that she couldn't have done it without the help and guidance she received from women such as noted Jungian psychotherapist and fellow panelist, Marion Woodman. And she was concerned about how other women who couldn't afford such professional guidance would be able to grapple with the issues that keep women from discovering themselves and becoming empowered.

I believe *Embracing Your Power Woman* is a tool to fill that need. As you explore this book, you will learn from your peers, other women whose stories become your guides, helpers, and confidants. And if you choose to join with a group of women to discuss the book and the exercises, your circle of guides, helpers, and confidants will expand to include all the stories of all the women in your group.

As was evident from the Women and Power Conference, all women, no matter what our age, are powerful. As younger women, our power is focused more in our Yin nature, and as we move into and through menopause, our power grows and deepens as it includes our Yang nature. In my fifties, I'm just hitting my stride. I feel like I've been preparing for this part of my life since adolescence.

This in no way detracts from the first half of my life, which was far from dreary or boring. I have been an actor, writer, dancer, mother (a single mom for the most part), and motion-picture production executive working in Los Angeles, New York, and Europe. I reared a terrific son and married three wonderful men. The third, whom I married at forty-five in the middle of my peri-menopause, was the charm. I studied metaphysics, have been on a spiritual path of healing and transformation for thirty years, and have a successful transformational healing practice. Having done all that, I still feel that I am just beginning to fly.

I believe all of us have a seed waiting deep within our souls that holds the key to our life's purpose. In adolescence we had glimpses of it. In this book and course we will reconnect with our teen years to rediscover that early vision of our life's purpose and reacquaint ourselves with the power we felt, however fleetingly, during that potent period of our lives. Though most of us have little or no memory of it, we all had immense surges of feminine power and potency as adolescents. Unfortunately, for the majority of us, it was immediately squelched. It was too heady, too strong, especially for that era. So we pushed it down. We ignored our power; we listened to our parents, and society. We became supportive girlfriends and then wives, even as we formed women's groups, shaped the feminist movement of the 1960s, and demanded equality. Many of us worked hard in the male-dominated work world, and we made great strides. But very few of us have achieved the level promised by that seed of purpose suppressed in adolescence.

Angeles Arrien says in her audio cassette *The Second Half of Life,* "We are born with a great dream for our lives, a dream which may have been submerged or derailed along the way by family or career realities. In the second half of life, after your roots have gone deeply into the world, it is time to resurrect this dream. For now, the blossom of your 'wild and precious life' is ready to bring forth the fruit of your unique and special creative gifts. By reclaiming your life dream—by refusing to stay down—you 'lift your heart up to heaven' and make all things possible."

In our youth, there was no definition of feminine power. To be powerful meant to be like men. Men's power is about power over others—and it is thus one of the reasons so many women shy away from the word "power."

Elizabeth Lesser opened the Women and Power Conference by saying, "This weekend we are asking the question, what does it mean when we put the words *women* and *power* in the same sentence?…and how do we change the power paradigm?" Later Eve Ensler described the new paradigm and women's power as both mystical and practical, saying, "[This new paradigm] power would not be about conquering, it would be about collaborating. It would not be about invading; it would be about inviting. It would not be about occupying; it would be about offering, inspiring, and serving."

In the women's movement of the 1960s and '70s, women looked at the world outside the home, realized we wanted to be part of it, and learned the rules and traditions of the male-dominated worlds of business and commerce and how to gain power over others. We were junior men in training. Some of us were able to adapt more easily than others, and gained levels of success based on that ability. Others of us struggled to fit into the uncomfortable mold of this kind of power and found marginal or little success.

This book and course are about discovering the true feminine power within us, the power that is not about power over, but the power of co-creating with others and the power within ourselves. The power of the feminine is immense. And it is this very immensity that created the patriarchal backlash five thousand years ago that has forced women to suppress their power ever since. The great goddess Inanna, the Sumerian goddess of the whole earth, who will be one of our guides throughout this book and course, represents the enormity of true feminine power—the power to create life, embrace death, overcome fear, and command the forces of destruction to relent, recede, and reform.

Aging comes to mind first as most of us contemplate moving into and past menopause. Aging in our western society is a time of endings. We retire. We give up our previous lives. Many move away from their long-time homes to huddle with other aging people. There is a sense of giving up. Being finished. And failing health is the great expectation of aging in the United States. Each little ache or pain reminds us that, "Yes, we're getting old." Psychological research shows that we get what we expect. Expect aches and pains to lead to dementia, cancer, or heart disease, and it's pretty certain that they will.

So why not change what you expect from this phase of your life and see what happens? Scary? Yes, it's a little scary, but there's not much in life that isn't at least somewhat frightening. And still, we go ahead. Deepak Chopra explains how it is our intention that dictates how our body ages. In *Ageless Body, Timeless Mind*, he says, "Because the mind influences every cell in the body, human aging is fluid and changeable; it can speed up, slow down, stop for a time, and even reverse itself. Hundreds of research findings over the past three decades have verified that aging is much more dependent on the individual than was ever dreamed of in the past. ...nothing holds more power over the body than the beliefs of the mind."

But, as Wayne Dyer tells us in *The Power of Intention*, that power of the mind or intention is not a "pit bull resolve," as we've so long believed, but rather the ability to connect to what Dyer describes as "the ominipresent power of intention." And in connecting to this universal intention with the power of our hearts and minds, we can create our own reality of aging.

My friend Elissa recently turned fifty. She has had a very exciting life. She's lived in LA, Italy, and New York. We met when she was twenty-six and working as a secretary for the head of a large motion-picture production company in Hollywood. She is an extremely beautiful woman and therefore found herself in relationships with several prominent film directors. And though she left Hollywood and found success selling real estate in New York City, it wasn't until a couple of years ago—when she made the transition from peri-menopause into menopause—that she allowed herself to listen to the inner voice that prompted her to find the seed of her true purpose.

At first she thought her inner voice was telling her to become a graphic artist, so she went back to college and majored in art. In art school, the voice that lay dormant during her younger years was allowed to get louder and louder. Finally, it got so loud, she could hear that graphic art wasn't what she longed for. Instead, she found that what would fulfill her purpose was filmmaking. Against all odds, she was accepted into the graduate film program at Columbia University. The beautiful young woman dated film directors. The beautiful older woman will direct films herself.

When I told Elissa about this book and the course, she told me to tell my students and readers that the hardest part is the fear. "Tell them to face the fear no matter how hard that is," she said, "because it's so worth it."

All I can add to Elissa's impassioned statement is that when you do face those fears and overcome them you will feel a pride that is sweeter than any feeling you've ever had.

The Eleven Points of Power, which this course is based on, came out of a lecture about creativity that I gave to a group of mid-life women just before I began teaching this course for the first time. To find the thread for the lecture, I played a game that I often give to my students. In this game you write a heading at the top of a piece of paper and then free-associate until you have a list of about ten subheadings. On this occasion, I wrote the heading *WOMEN AND CREATIVITY.* Quickly, I scribbled down a list of subheadings—*motherhood, nurturing, home, love, capability, intuition, understanding, partnership,* and *community.* I was a mid-life woman myself, and when I read the list, I could feel something missing. Something more powerful. I played the game again. This time, I added another word to the heading, and I began free-associating under the heading *OLDER WOMEN AND CREATIVITY.* I was amazed to see how different this list was: *direction, frustration, ability, health, money, power, worldliness, leadership, success,* and *freedom.* From this new list, I shaped that first talk. Over the next few years, as I developed this course in women's circles, the original eleven subheadings evolved into the Eleven Points of Power, which we will work with in this book and course. They are:

- *The Power of Self Love*
- *The Power of Creativity*
- *The Power of Self Trust*
- *The Power of Courage and Ability*
- *The Power of Health and Beauty*
- *The Power of True Wealth*
- *The Power of Our Own Direction*
- *The Power of Partnership and Community*
- *The Power of Authentic Leadership*
- *The Power of Enlightened Success*
- *The Power of Freedom*

In this book and course, we will make the journey through the Eleven Points of Power to become initiated into the next step of our lives and to embrace our innate feminine power. As we meet the challenge of this transition together as sisters, we will dive past resistance, down to our true worth. And once we've found it we will excavate it, bring it into the light, revel in it, and prepare ourselves for our powerful new life as Power Women.

This course can be done alone or in a circle. A circle is simply a group of women who meet in the spirit of sisterhood to share their hopes, fears, losses, successes, ideas, and joys in an atmosphere of respect, honor, loving, caring, and sharing.

Jean Shinoda Bolen, M.D., in her book *The Millionth Circle*, says, "…women as a gender have a natural talent for [circles]. The circle is an archetypal form that feels familiar to the psyches of most women. It's personal and egalitarian."

Women work well in this kind of environment. Our learning and growth is often triggered when we hear the stories of other women's similar life experiences. Doing this work in a circle gives you the opportunity to heal and grow in a safe, supportive space, so that when you have completed the course you will feel ready to step out of the circle into the larger community, with the power of true sisterhood as a foundation.

At Omega's Women and Power Conference, Gloria Steinem said that it was time for us to make our "declaration of *interdependence*." She said that in the 1950s we were dependent, in the '60s and '70s we declared our independence, and now it is time for us to become interdependent.

Eventually I see all of us—women and men—living and working interdependently. But to learn and begin to embody the possibilities of such a bold and exciting next step, we must first learn to be interdependent with our sisters. Together, women can cause powerful positive change throughout the planet. As we do, we will be cutting a new path for the women who come behind us.

If you decide to do the work in a circle, it's good to be aware that all the women who choose to journey through the Eleven Points of Power are different people with different dreams, different purposes, different desires, different ages, and in different stages of their menopausal passage. Some of you won't even have begun it, some will have completed it, and others may be right in the middle of it. Some will have children at home, some will have grown children, and others may have never been parents. But what everyone has in common is that we are all women in the second half of life and we are all women with a future.

Many women fear close interaction with other women, because they have been wounded in the past. Peri-menopausal women can feel especially vulnerable as they experience themselves dumped unceremoniously into this unknown world. Older or more secure women need to reach out to help our younger or less seasoned sisters to feel safe and honored in their process.

As Power Women in or beginning the second half of life, we are part of a new sisterhood. As sisters united, we can work miracles. The world needs our wisdom and our strength. Our communities need our vision, and we need to express our gifts.

We are living in an era of exciting transformation. And although this is sometimes difficult to believe while we're reeling from constant media reports of war, terrorism, executions, torture, and retribution, many women are nevertheless feeling a new sense of feminine power emerging along the subtle waves of awareness. And this translates into the belief that there is another way to live together. I think many of us know that, if given the chance, we could suggest and even execute programs that could lead us out of this worldwide cycle of violence toward a more loving, caring, and nurturing society.

"I believe that to meet the challenges of our times, human beings will have to develop a greater sense of universal responsibility. Each of us must learn to work not just for oneself, one's own family or nation, but also for the benefit of all humankind. Universal responsibility is the key to human survival. It is the best foundation for world peace."

– His Holiness the Dalai Lama

Women across the globe are sick and tired of having their sons, and daughters, brothers, sisters, husbands, lovers, and strangers slaughtered in senseless violence—whether in war or on the city streets. A concentrated effort focused on healing is needed now by a large segment of the population skilled at organization, diplomacy, nurturing, decision-making, budgeting, scheduling, and crisis management. Where can we find people who have all these qualifications?

The answer is simple: women in the second half of life.

You can't raise a family, handle a career, and maintain relationships over thirty-odd years without becoming mighty proficient in these areas. Feminine wisdom is needed to carry the world through today's chaos and into the next age. What the world needs now are powerful, wise, courageous, compassionate women who will step up to the boys and tell them to sit down, shut up, and listen to their mothers.

Women in the second half of life are the greatest untapped natural resource on the planet. We are plentiful and getting more so by the day as the Baby Boomer generation ages. As we women in the second half of life learn to honor our wisdom, we will be able to make sweeping changes in our society while simultaneously having a helluva good time.

I envision Power Women as a great force for good in this world. I see us sitting around chatting and weaving the fabric of a new and more hopeful society. Though the idea of women chatting is often viewed as frivolous, I believe that when we chat about the things that matter to us, our families, our pain, our healing, our emotional growth, our dreams, and desires for ourselves, our communities, and our world, that the focus we bring through the act of chatting has the power to create change. I see us using all the wisdom we've gathered over the past forty, fifty, sixty, or more years to step into our true destinies. I see us working as partners to heal ourselves, our communities, our countries, and our Earth.

I believe we can do this by healing our inner adolescent girls, bringing them up to speed with our Power Women selves, and in so doing discovering our true paths with grace and ease. I see us grappling with our monsters together. I see us healing each other and helping each other see the true beauty within all of us. Finding and owning our true power is a daunting task that takes courage. But are you ready to spend the next twenty, thirty, or more years, succumbing to society's stereotype of the post-menopausal woman? Someone said recently that post-menopausal women would make good cat burglars because no one sees us or notices us. Do you want to be invisible? Or do you want to screw up your courage and embrace your power? The owning of our power is exhilarating. I hope I can help you find joy in this amazing process of healing, growth, enlightenment, and empowerment.

BECOMING ACQUAINTED WITH

The Eleven Points of Power

"Some went among women who were alone, teaching them to join together, for there is hope in two women, help in three women, strength in four, joy in five, power in six, and against seven, no gate may stand."

– Sherri S. Tepper

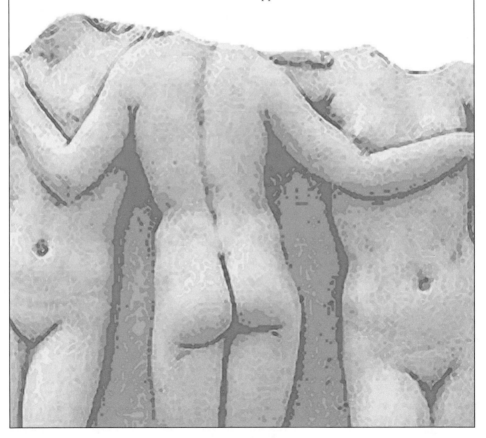

The journey to embracing and embodying our Power Women has eleven steps, the Eleven Points of Power. These points of power will reveal a potential you have known existed all your life, but were not sure exactly when and how it could be fulfilled.

Now is the time. In the first half of our lives, we laid the groundwork for this journey to embody this new powerful self. Now it's time to elevate all our knowledge, life experience, and wisdom to the next level. We will discover a new kind of woman: not the mother, not the pre-menopausal career woman, not the seducer, but a brand-new woman. We will incorporate those parts of ourselves we deem still relevant to our lives and discard those we feel are irrelevant. This brand-new woman has some age on her, but she is not yet "old." She has wisdom, but she is not yet Crone. She has ideas, and she has plans.

The peri-menopausal and menopausal years can be difficult, and as we make the transition and emerge on the other side we tend to feel a bit wobbly. We may have some great thoughts and feelings about what we want, but no road map to follow.

At the onset of adolescence we all had at least a fleeting vision of ourselves as powerful women. That vision was muted or even silenced in most women by our parents, our peers, and our society. Now, at midlife, with a huge cache of experience, we have the skills to reconnect to that original vision's powerful potential.

With each of life's passages, we must pass through an initiation. In menopause we find ourselves descending into a dark initiation that, for many women, can seem brutal and pointless, until we recognize that all we are being asked to do is to surrender the trappings of our childbearing years in order to take on the garments of our Power Woman. Having survived this initiation and become aware of its purpose, we can accept our new role in society and play it out to its fullest potential. This course is an initiatory process, which will help you consciously experience your transition as you come of age in the second half of life.

EMBRACING TRUE FEMININE POWER

The word *power* is difficult for many women to embrace, because power in our present day society is considered to mean having power over others for the purpose of control. But the first definition of power in Webster's New Collegiate Dictionary is "The ability or capacity to perform effectively." The second definition is "A specific capacity, faculty, or aptitude, e.g., *strong decisive powers*" [my italics]. The third is "Strength or force exerted or capable of being exerted." It isn't until the fourth definition that we encounter the word used to express *power over*. Further down the list at number seven, is "Effectiveness: forcefulness (e.g. *a film of extraordinary power*)."

Looking at the word power through the lens of these definitions gives us a new sense of what feminine power can be. But feminine power can also be frightening to women and men because it reminds us of the raw power of the primal feminine, the Mother Earth and Her powerful storms, seas, earthquakes, and volcanoes. Ancient feminine power was what maintained the species in the wilderness before humans began to exert power over Nature and attempted to harness Her through the act of civilization— creating boundaries, damming rivers and streams, cutting down forests.

Feminine power is raw energy. It is awe-inspiring. It is the fierceness of a woman protecting her children. It is the strength of women working together to create safe communities, schools, healing environments, and an ecologically healthy planet. It's about having the strength and courage to stand for the good and against the bad. Feminine Power is *your* power. Own it.

As we prepare to take the journey to embrace our Power Women we must first understand some of the characteristics of a Power Woman. They are not meant to intimidate you, but offered as food for thought. As you make your journey you will undoubtedly refine and add to this list.

- *A Power Woman is loving, wise, honest, and caring.*
- *A Power Woman embodies courage and integrity.*
- *A Power Woman loves and honors herself, her family, her sisters, her community, and the world.*
- *A Power Woman is a seeker on the path of Spirit.*
- *A Power Woman is an activist for good on the Earth.*

THE ELEVEN POINTS OF POWER

In numerology, eleven is the first master number. Eleven also becomes a two when the ones are added together. Two is the number of the feminine. As women (two) in the second half of life, we are reaching our mastery (eleven).

Each of the Eleven Points of Power is a step on the road to uncovering, recovering, and reconnecting to the original seed of our potential power and the development of our inner strength. In this book, each Point of Power has a chapter devoted to it that includes essays, anecdotes, and games/exercises to help us mine the treasures that lie hidden in our hearts and souls. After the mining comes the polishing, then the fine-tuning.

HOW TO USE THIS BOOK

This book is a course. It is meant to be *done*, as well as to be read. You can do it on your own or in a circle of women. The power of women is heightened greatly when we cluster in groups. Therefore, I recommend creating an intimate circle of women in your community or even on the Internet to join you on this journey. Remember the quote at the beginning of this chapter: "Some went among women who were alone, teaching them to join together, for there is hope in two women, help in three women, strength in four, joy in five, power in six, and against seven, no gate may stand." Try to have at least seven women in your circle, but any number is fine. (See Appendix I, "Guidelines for Forming A Circle.")

Whether you're doing this course alone or in a circle you will want to look through the book carefully and thoroughly to note how the chapters are laid out. Each is designed to be studied for one week. There are Eleven Points of Power, so there are eleven chapters to be done for eleven weeks, plus one extra week for a ceremony and celebration.

At the beginning of each week, read the essays in the chapter. You should be able to read the entire chapter up to the Games and Exercises section in no more than two sittings. You will want to have a pen and paper next to you so that you can scribble notes in the "Questions to

Ponder" sections of the chapter. It's important to linger over the "Questions to Ponder." They will take you deeper into your subconscious to promote very important growth.

After you have read the chapter, spend the rest of the week doing the games and exercises. **Remember to look over the list of games and exercises at the beginning of the week, so that you can plan ahead for anything that may take time.** If you leave the games and exercises until the last minute, they won't have a chance to make the subconscious changes they're meant to accomplish.

Additionally, there are two tools that are used consistently throughout the course. These are meditating and journaling. They are explained fully in "Week One – The Power of Self Love." The games and exercises are designed to help you dive down into the dark and murky waters that separate you from the light of your soul. The meditation and journaling tools help you swim up out of the dark into the clear, illuminated waters of your true soul path.

Sometimes the games will seem frivolous, unrelated, or even silly, but forge ahead anyway. They work below everyday awareness. There is magic in this work, and magic acts in the realm of our intuition. As women in the second half of life, our intuition is enhanced. In *The Wisdom of Menopause*, Dr. Christiane Northrop tells us that during the hormonal changes of menopause, a switch is turned on in the temporal lobes of the brain that actually amplifies our intuitive brain functions. The less rational games and exercises in the chapters are created to sharpen this newly ignited intuition.

Also, I particularly recommend you read the following three books to give you a rich background for the course:

- *The Chalice and the Blade* – by Rianne Eisler
- *The Alphabet Versus the Goddess* – by Leonard Shlain
- *The Wisdom of Menopause* – by Christiane Northrup, M.D.

There are other books in the bibliography you may also find useful.

A JOURNEY IS A CHALLENGE WITH GREAT REWARDS ALONG THE WAY

"It must be understood that taking care of the planet will be done as we take care of ourselves. You know that you can't really make much of a difference in things until you change yourself."

– Alice Walker

You will experience many extreme emotional highs and lows when reading the essays and working with the tools, games, and exercises. They are designed for just that purpose. Some weeks you'll think that life is good and the world is a magnificent place. Other weeks you'll experience depression, anger, or deep grief. Some weeks you'll be confused by a combination of joy and sadness as you wind your way through your memories. But don't be afraid. This emotional roller coaster can't hurt you. The emotions are just the shadows of long past events rising to the surface, to be acknowledged, embraced, and released.

Over the course of our lives we have collected a great deal of baggage that must be discarded so we can move into this wondrous new era. These are, as Shakespeare wrote, "The slings and arrows of outrageous fortune." The arrows are lodged firmly in our backs, our hearts, our minds, and our wombs. They have poison tips, and the poison continues to seep into our emotional systems. In the process of this course, you may become tired of extracting arrows. You may find yourself saying, "Forget this!" You won't want to turn another page, read another essay, answer another question, or play another stupid game. Please do it anyway. It will change your life. Yes, of course, the initial removal of these arrows can be, will be, painful. But the relief, once your system has had time to adjust to their absence, is pure ecstasy.

When you feel the sting of the arrows take a tip from transformational facilitator, Marianne Weidlein, who tells us

"Smile the deepest, warmest love into your heart,
and draw enough power from this high frequency
to dispel whatever life brings your way."

Visit her website at www.empoweringvision.com

Each chapter is designed to be accomplished in one week, so that the beginning of each chapter is like a fresh new start. Some chapters will be harder than others. Some chapters will be just plain fun. Once you begin the process, don't stop. It's important to move to each next step in a week-by-week progression. If the emotions you encounter seem thorny one week, the next week will take you in a completely new direction, which will bring new insights. As you progress, you will begin finding a new sense of yourself and your personal power.

Within a circle, each person will experience highs and lows at different parts of the course. We all come to the circle with different life stories. That's the great thing about doing this work with other women. When some of us are down, others are up. Those who are having a great week need to be mindful of your sisters who may be facing the darker emotional lows. Each member of the circle is there to gently remind the others that this is a journey. And journeys of any value are never smooth. Great journeys are traveled along roads with unexpected twists and turns. The evil wizard may capture you for a while, but using your ingenuity and perseverance you will escape and continue on.

Remember: we are all beautiful, fantastic women, in the process of removing obstacles in our paths. As in any exciting quest, each leg of the journey leaves the previous adventures and misadventures behind. And so it is with the Eleven Points of Power. At the beginning of each chapter, the previous week's work is left behind, and you embark upon a brand-new phase filled with a whole new set of challenges, revelations, surprises, and rewards. At times it may seem as if you're slipping backward, but if you do the work as it is designed to be done—reading the essays and answering the questions at the beginning of the week, playing the games throughout the week, and practicing journaling and meditation daily—you will move steadily forward toward the final point of power, which is Freedom. I recommend that you put a sticky note at the beginning of this section, "A Journey is a Challenge with Many Rewards Along the Way," and refer to it whenever you're finding it difficult to proceed. Also, if you are in a circle, you may want to reread this section out loud during your weekly circle meetings.

GUIDELINES FOR FRIENDSHIPS AND CIRCLES

"We are all longing to go home to some place we have never been—a place, half-remembered, and half-envisioned… Somewhere, there are people to whom we can speak with passion…. Somewhere a circle of hands will open to receive us, eyes will light up as we enter, voices will celebrate with us whenever we come into our own power. Arms to hold us when we falter. A circle of healing. A circle of friends."   – Starhawk

One of the gifts of doing this course is that it was originally designed to be done within a circle of women. It is well documented that loneliness is one of the main causes of depression. Women, either in or out of marriages or primary relationships, can find themselves lonely without a circle of women friends. In the second half of life, women friends become even more important. But lack of training or bad training often makes it difficult for women to create lasting friendships. Here are some simple guidelines that can help in forming a circle of women friends.

The first rule of any true friendship is non-judgment. We have all had very different lives. We've all done wonderful things and we have all made some mistakes. Let us not judge one another, but realize that we are sisters on the path toward our magnificence.

No one needs to be "fixed." Your sister across the circle is on her own unique life path. She will grow and evolve exactly as she should. When she talks of her personal challenges, we should never assume that we are being asked to fix her. We should never assume that we *can* fix her, or for that matter, that there is anything which needs to be fixed. Each one of us has challenges to face and embrace. As we listen to a sister's story, we may recognize our own challenges, some of which we may have overcome ourselves. But our solutions will not necessarily be another's solutions. At times it may be appropriate to offer our past experiences in order to express empathy, but never to demonstrate how someone else can be fixed.

Learning to listen is one of life's greatest lessons. The Native Americans share in their circles with a Talking Stick. Many others are becoming aware of this practice and using it in their groups. As many of you know, a Talking Stick is a stick or any object that is passed around the circle and held by whomever wishes to speak. While the Talking Stick is in the hand of the speaker, everyone must give her complete attention to that speaker. No one is allowed to interrupt until the speaker relinquishes the stick. Though this is a wonderful device, it can't work unless everyone in the circle shows respect. Therefore, no one should hold the stick longer than is absolutely necessary to make her particular point. But while she has it, the others are asked to focus and listen with total attention. If, while another woman is speaking, we are planning our argument or thinking of the story we want to tell, then we are disrespectful and will also miss what the other person is saying.

Fear keeps us from truly listening to someone else. There are many kinds of fear. It can be masked in the guise of self-doubt, competition, arrogance, or anxiety—the fear that we won't be prepared when it's our turn to speak, the fear that our story or opinion will not be heard, the fear that someone else will steal the spotlight, the fear that we will not be acknowledged as being better than someone else. When we can drop these fears, knowing that we will say exactly what we need to say when our turn comes, we will be able to listen with our hearts and our minds to our sisters.

The final guideline is to avoid drama and gossip. When engaging in transformational work as we do in this course, it is imperative to uncover our old memories, experience whatever pain they elicit, process that pain, assimilate the essence, and move on.

Frequently people recall a painful memory and immediately seek someone who will listen to each horrible circumstance of their story. Instead of taking the memory into their journaling and meditation where they can look at it, dive down into the depths of it, and then give it over to the light, they wallow in the drama of it. This is extremely counter-productive. In *Anatomy of the Spirit*, Caroline Myss warns that support groups too often keep people from healing, because the members become so comfortable in the process of sharing their pain with supportive others, that they never heal. She calls this "woundology."

I have found that telling our stories over and over keeps us on the very surface of the pain. We must go deep below the surface to find the way out of the pain. And this we must do alone. Without diving into the muck in the privacy of our own consciousness, we cannot retrieve the gems of wisdom awaiting us. A circle of women friends can lovingly encourage each other to go deeper, and still refrain from advancing each other's melodramas or promoting "woundology."

COMMITTING TO YOUR POWER WOMAN

The coming weeks can be one of the most dynamic periods of your life, but you must make the commitment to do the work. You will get as much out of this work as you put into it. The essays, questions, tools, games, and exercises are all designed to take you on an amazing journey of self-discovery to embrace your Power Woman. Take a moment right now to commit to this course, to doing all the required reading, and all the games, exercises, and tools. I assure you that if you do, you will be rewarded in ways that you cannot even imagine.

If you feel unsure of yourself, try filling out and signing the contract below to help you fully commit to this powerful initiation.

CONTRACT WITH MYSELF

I,_____, am ready and willing to begin my journey to discover and embody my own Power Woman. I,_____, commit to doing all the reading, meditation, journaling, and games for each of the Eleven Points of Power. I, _____, am aware that this is a guided spiritual journey that will take me deep into my consciousness for the purpose of transformation, and I commit to focusing my mind, my heart, and my spirit on this course to its completion.

_____(Signature)

_____(Date)

Remember to look back at the section called "A Journey is a Challenge with Great Rewards Along the Way," whenever you feel resistance to continuing the work. It will help you refocus and get over the rough spots.

You are a Power Woman ready to emerge from your chrysalis. Begin the journey now!

THE POWER OF

Self-Love

"Love yourself first and everything else falls into line.
You really have to love yourself to get anything done in this world."

– Lucille Ball

The foundation of a Power Woman is her own self-love. Without self-love we have nothing to build upon. We are unanchored, adrift, and afraid. To be a Power Woman, we must have, first and foremost, the courage to look inward. As we travel into our inner landscapes we will find our strengths and weaknesses. We will learn to give up judgment and simply embrace the complex and amazing persons we are. Self-love is a romance with self. It has all the ups and downs of any relationship, but in the end, when we finally do fall in love with ourselves, we will be in a relationship that will last for the rest of our lives. Lovers exude and attract love. As self-lovers we will do the same. And the more we open to recognize our goodness the more goodness we will have to share. As Power Women we can help reshape the world. To do that we must embrace that new shape within ourselves. And that shape is Love.

To become deeply acquainted with our self-love we must revisit adolescence, because it is at some point during those early transitional years that young women experience deep self-love. Although many of us can't remember the feeling, for at least a brief moment we all knew who we were. We envisioned a brilliant future, and we loved ourselves. We loved our developing bodies. Our developing personalities had a sense of the heroic in them. We were on top of the world.

But too quickly, that glorious sense of self was quelled. Stifled. Stopped. We were told not to dream big dreams. Not to be selfish. Not to be all that we knew we were. And to some degree we all succumbed to the pressures of our families and society. My dear friend, the journalist and poet Judy Simmons, wrote to me recently, remembering our teenage years together, "We were talented, naïve, gutsy, passionate, and, above all, conscious—so in love with life. Who knew how hard it gets?" At midlife many of us can relate to Judy's sentiment. We have all been challenged in many ways during the first half of our lives. But it was these life challenges that created the strong women we are today. Even when we feel weakened by the biological, emotional, and mental changes our bodies go through in peri-menopause and menopause, it is important to remember that these very changes are the fuel that will produce our Power Women.

Much the same thing happened in adolescence when changing hormones knocked us around like popcorn in a hot pan and gave birth to our childbearing selves. The one big difference is that we had little or no awareness of what was happening to us back then, but now we have the opportunity to be conscious and aware. If you are reading this book, you have made the decision to be a proactive participant in your life and your emerging Power Woman. That is a fundamental step toward real self-love.

At the Women and Power Conference in New York, Sally Field was one of the speakers. The crowd of over 1200 women adored her. Though many of the other speakers had elicited a great deal of excitement, there was a very special quality to the way we responded to Sally. As I listened to her tell of her own personal struggles, I realized that most of the women in the room had grown up with Sally Field as Gidget and the Flying Nun, and through her we were collectively reconnecting to our teenage-selves.

We also remembered her as the powerful grown woman character of Norma Rae, and the private person who at the Academy Awards uttered the sentiment, "You like me. You really, really, like me." This deeply felt statement engendered a great deal of criticism in the press, but we women understood all too well the insecurity that provoked it. Sally Field connected our lives for us, linking us to both our adolescent and our Power Women selves.

Although I had the good fortune to raise a son, I didn't have the pleasure of parenting a daughter. But I know many mothers of daughters, and I have heard again and again how difficult teenage girls can be. I was a very difficult teenager myself. Being a difficult teenage girl seems to me to be a direct result of reaching that point in our lives when we suddenly experience our personal power and are immediately told to shut it off. Some teenage girls are vocal about their discontent, others suffer in silence, but we all do suffer from this denial of our personal power.

Most boys, on the other hand, are encouraged to be all they can be. They are told that to be selfish is important if they are going to succeed in the world. They are told to: *Dream the big dream! Go for the gusto! Live life to the fullest! Seize the day.*

In the 1950s, '60s, '70s, and even into the '80s, many girls were told: *Don't act too smart or the boys won't like you! Be quiet and let the boy do the talking! Lose the game, the contest, the argument!* And there were more subtle ways that we learned from society to keep the secret of our power under wraps until we could sublimate it completely with the duties of motherhood. We were expected to act like ladies, not to talk too loud, and not to make too much of an issue of things we felt strongly about.

Instead of learning self-love, we learned that to become a good woman we needed to love and be loved by others, to be supportive of others, to care for others, always to put others first. We knew from earliest childhood that we were expected to become wives and mothers. Even today, forty years into the second wave of feminism, our society still considers other ambitions to be additional and secondary to our main jobs as wives and mothers. Our dreams and desires outside the home were considered super-fluous and often just plain ridiculous.

Of course, our biology is also responsible for our roles as mothers in the first half of our lives, and motherhood is a wonderful, fulfilling, and necessary part of female life, as fatherhood is of male life. Those of us who chose to stay at home and raise our children and leave the career until later, will be happily surprised to find that becoming a Power Woman entails finding meaningful and fulfilling work in the second half of life. It's the denial of our dreams and desires that we are addressing here. Each part of our lives deserves to be honored and revered, whether it is as a parent, a career woman, a grandmother, a Power Woman or a Crone. And because few of us have experience in being honored for our roles as women, we have to learn to do it for ourselves by being our own mothers and mentors now.

I wanted to be an actress. That was the silliest thing my parents had ever heard. They laughed and scoffed whenever I brought it up. I tried to ignore their ridicule. I went to auditions and got parts in plays in the local theatres. I became an apprentice and eventually a featured performer in the local professional summer stock company. One evening after dinner my father was in a bad temper, so he arbitrarily grounded me. When I

explained that I had dress rehearsal for a play that was opening the following night, he waved me away and refused to change his mind. My
mother had to beg him for an hour, until he finally relented and allowed
me to go.

Even though I was the kind of girl who fought and screamed and
refused to have my dream stifled, and even though I went to college and
majored in drama and subsequently went to Hollywood, the scars of the
scoffing and lack of support were etched into my subconscious, holding me
back from fully achieving my deepest desires. My story is just one of the
millions about women who were stopped just as they were about to bud
into magnificent blooms.

Questions to Ponder

- *Can you remember a moment when you felt you could conquer the world?*
- *Did you have support from your family for your adolescent dreams?*
- *Did you ever confide your adolescent dreams to anyone? If you did, what was
  the response?*

Though my mother sometimes took my side, as in the story about the
rehearsal, she had very little self-love, and therefore she couldn't sustain
that kind of support for long. Society, or my dad, quickly reminded her that
girls had a place, and I needed to learn mine. My brother experienced life
with my parents in a completely different way. He remembers their constant support, their unfailing belief in him and in his dreams and ambitions.

As I describe this phase of life that was stifling for so many of us, I am
reminded of how much we have overcome. Our generation was on the
front lines of the second wave of the women's movement. We made great
strides. We stepped into what was once an all-male job market. We cracked
the glass ceiling. But as individual human beings, we are still held back by
the lack of initial support for our true powerful natures. In addition, many
of us who stepped into the business world, found there was a different set

of rules for the women. We had to play the game by the men's rules, but without the same entitlement. Even as some of us tried to be tough like the guys, we were reminded in subtle and not-so-subtle ways that we were women. And if we became too forceful we got the reputation of being bitches, ball-breakers, or worse.

We can never change the era in which we were raised or the way our parents, our teachers, and our peers treated us. But by using the games and exercises in this book, we can go back in time to rescue our teenage girl and bring her dreams, her ambitions, and her inner truths up to speed with the Power Women we are becoming. We can become the loving, support-ive parent of this teenage girl. We can instill in her a deep sense of self-love and self-respect. We can look at her dreams and ambitions with love. We can help her stand up against that old-fashioned society and say: *"Move out of my way. I have some important things to do. I have interesting ideas to share, art that needs to be created, science that needs to be explored, ecological changes that need to be enforced, music that needs to played, books that need to be written, political offices that need to be won!"*

NURTURING OURSELVES SO THAT WE MAY BE BORN AGAIN

"We can only learn to love by loving."

– Iris Murdoch

For the majority of women the process of peri-menopause and menopause begins somewhere in our forties and ends somewhere in our fifties. There is nothing *uniform* about the change. Rather, this profound transition is nothing short of chaotic. Little is known medically about menopause, because researchers must make everything conform to invent-ed standards that can be tested, and women's bodies and psyches reject such efforts.

As we face this new half of life with no blueprints, no road maps, no guidelines, we are necessarily afraid. And the fact that we are having night sweats, hot flashes, and losing our memories doesn't help our self-esteem. Terrified and alone, with bodies acting like they have never acted before, we flounder. We try to find answers by examining the past, but none of the old ways work.

The one thing we have always been able to fall back on is our ability to nurture. But for many women at this time of life there is no one to nurture. For many, the children are grown; for others, there have never been children; for still others, the husband they have nurtured for so long is suffering his own mid-life crisis, sometimes with devastating consequences. The majority of husbands simply have no idea what's going on.

We run in circles, chasing our tails, trying to find ways to stop what seems to be a downward spiral into darkness and futility. This is when we should call on our instinct to nurture. But instead of reaching out to help others now we must turn the nurturing inward. We must mother ourselves. Because in the downward spiraling there is an end, and that end is the birth of a new human being. Ourselves!

Because of our cultural role as nurturers of others, the mere idea of loving and mothering ourselves (even to the exclusion of others) can feel anarchical, subversive. But this is exactly what we must do. We must love ourselves selfishly, the way we loved our babies when they were tiny. We must nestle ourselves into our own bosoms and suckle ourselves, until we're ready to emerge as magnificent Power Women. For women who still have small children during the years of menopause, the challenge is to find a way to balance self-nurturing with child nurturing. But this is not a time for nurturing a man. Men need to become self-sufficient and even to become nurturers. Hopefully, as men in the second half of life come to embrace and express the Yin side of their natures, this will become part of their role in society.

Lisa, a forty-five year old mother of three children under the age of five, and who until the birth of her children was a successful marketing executive, was offered a good job in a PR firm thirty miles from her home. The family needed the income, and Lisa felt that she was ready to step back into the business world after several years of being a stay-at-home mom. She accepted the job and made the preparations necessary for child-care.

The night before her first day back at work, she looked at what she was about to do to her life. She would be gone from her family twelve-and-a-half hours a day. She would be working for someone else, and she would be exhausted most of the time. She was horrified at these prospects. The job made good economic sense, but that was the only kind of sense it made. At 1 a.m. on the day she was supposed to appear for her first day of work she sat with her husband and explained that as much as they needed the money, she could not do this to herself. As she told me about her decision to stay at home with her children and find publicity work she could do from home and be her own boss, I heard the voice of her Power Woman, the voice of self-love, sounding loud and clear. She is also lucky enough to have a loving husband who was in complete agreement with her decision.

Questions to Ponder

- *When was the last time you were nurtured by anyone?*
- *Do you think you are lovable?*
- *Have you ever considered mothering yourself? How would you go about it?*

THE GODDESS INANNA

In ancient Mesopotamia (modern-day Iraq) the mythical goddess Inanna was Queen of the Land. She took every king as her bridegroom. Her blood flowed in every stream, lake, river, and ocean. She was the earth itself. But, although Inanna was queen of the world and wife of the handsome Dumuzi and all the kings of the Earth, she grew restless after a time and decided to journey to the underworld to visit her sister Ereshkigal, the goddess of death. As Inanna prepared for her descent she was aware of how dangerous this trip would be, so she gave her assistant, Ninshubur, instructions about how to implement a rescue mission should she fail to return.

At last Inanna was ready to leave. She made her descent through the seven gates of the underworld before she reached the home of her sister. At each gate she was commanded to strip off a piece of her regal clothing and relinquish it to the gatekeeper. At last, ushered through the seventh gate and into the inner sanctum, she stood totally naked and vulnerable, awaiting the reunion with her dear sister. She waited for hours until, at last, Ereshkigal arrived. Inanna opened her arms to embrace her sister, but before any words of greeting, Ereshkigal, the goddess of death, stabbed Inanna, killing her instantly. Ereshkigal hanged Inanna's body on a meat hook and left her there to rot.

As you make this journey to find your dark sister-self and all the power she holds for you, know that it is your own self-love that propels you into the darkness; and it is that same self-love that will eventually lift you to heights you've never dreamed imaginable.

As our childbearing bodies give way to our Power Women bodies, we are experiencing a death within. The journey strips us of our old garments and leaves us lifeless in the dark as our Power Woman self gestates. This is a time of immense transformation. Don't fear it. Embrace it.

You sisters who are starting the trip into the underworld, look to your older sisters who have traversed the darkness and returned, ready to become all they can be. Together, we will embrace the darkness, open to our own power through the Eleven Points of Power. With deep self-love and self-nurturing, we will discover our own, unique path for the next phase of our lives.

THE TOOLS

Hormones are the biological impetus driving us into new phases of our lives. In our youths, hormones drove us from childhood to adolescence to adult-hood. Now hormones drive us from childbearing women, to menopausal women, to Power Women. Since we have all been through the hormonal trans-formations of youth, it is only natural that we return to that period to find clues to help us through this change. As we re-discover the teenage girl still living in each of us, we will become her mother. As she feels our love, she will rise to the occasion and become our partner and our guide. In the Demeter/Persephone myth Demeter goes into the underworld to bring her lovely daughter Persephone back to Earth each spring. You will be playing the role of Demeter to your teenage Persephone, as you dive into your memory to find her, and bring her sorrows and her dreams into the light.

Our teenage girl may not be easy to find; she may be buried deep in the subconscious. To discover her we need tools. Meditation and journaling are our two main tools. These tools work as a team. The journaling opens our consciousness and leads us to new discoveries about our hidden selves. The meditation heals the wounds and allows us to enter heightened levels of con-scious awareness.

If we use these tools with the intention of being honest with ourselves in a non-judgmental way we will develop self-awareness. Self-awareness is the key to unlocking the past, and preparing the way for the future.

The tools work most effectively when you begin with the journaling and follow immediately with the meditation. And it is most successful when done first thing in the morning before breakfast.

JOURNALING

Journaling in this course may be different from other forms you have done in the past. This is the stripping-down process Inanna endures as she moves through the seven levels of the underworld. We must, like Inanna, get down to the skin, the meat, and the bones of our innermost selves. It is here we find our true selves, and can begin the love affair.

We call this kind of journaling stream-of-consciousness. It is done with no structure whatsoever. You simply pick up your pen or pencil and begin to write. During the first week you may get yourself going by writing a starting sentence such as "What does self-love mean?" or "Don't I have plenty of self-love?" or simply "I can't think of anything to write. This is a waste of time." Whatever sentence pops into your mind.

When we first wake up, we are halfway between the waking and sleeping state. We are still connected to the subconscious. And this is why it is so important to journal first thing after waking. It's at this time of the day when we can arouse more memories from the depths of our psyches than at any other time.

(**NOTE:** You may need a cup of coffee or tea, but try to get your hot drink with little or preferably no interaction with others in your household.)

Once you have written your first sentence, continue writing for approximately twenty minutes without stopping. This should come out to be at least three pages on 8 1/2" x 11" lined paper. If you reach three pages in less than twenty minutes, you can stop. If you have not finished three pages by the end of twenty minutes, continue writing until you have completed them.

William James introduced stream-of-consciousness writing in 1890 in his book *The Principles of Psychology*. James Joyce elevated stream-of-consciousness to a high place in literature in *Ulysses* and *Finnegan's Wake*. Virginia Woolf adapted the technique in *Mrs. Dalloway*, *To the Lighthouse*, and *The Waves*. The original concept was based on the Freudian understanding that ideas, and consciousness in general, are fluid and shifting rather than fixed, and that by writing without conscious intention, the mind is freed to allow the subconscious to surface effortlessly in an undetermined way.

This simply means that you write whatever comes out of your hand and onto the paper. Don't try to compose. Write only the feelings, thoughts, insights, or just plain garbage that spills, leaks, or flows out. The hand writes, not the mind. When you allow the hand to write and let the mind rest, the most amazing things can come forth. Don't worry about punctuation. Don't try to be profound. I can't emphasize this enough. Profundity may appear some days, but it will not come from trying, it will come from the very depths of your soul, and the only way for this to happen is to get out of the way and allow it onto the page. By writing pages and pages of what you consider garbage, dreck, nonsense, and babbling, you begin to unclog the channel that connects you directly to your inner divine-self, and when you do this she will begin to speak. But she won't be pushed.

Your journal is for your eyes only. Keep it in a safe place where no one else will read it. This is your place to talk about anything and anyone in anyway that you need to or want to. Don't sabotage yourself by leaving it out for others to read. When you begin a personal journal you are creating a safe place for all your feelings and thoughts. So keep it secure.

MEDITATION

As soon as you have completed your journaling, it is time to meditate. You have stirred the pot with your writing. Your pen is like a long pole that you plunge into a pond—a pond that seems clear and calm on the surface, but that has layers of dirt, sand, scum, and creatures living below. Your pen dislodges old barnacles, allows long-forgotten debris to float to the surface. Now you will use your "light energy" meditation to clear away this newly stirred up psychic waste and replace it with light.

The Light Energy Meditation is the single most important tool in this course. Don't leave it out. The light heals and transforms where nothing else can. Meditate alone daily, and always begin your weekly circle with this meditation. This will create a safe and loving lighted energy field where people will feel free to share.

Many people shy away from meditation. The idea of sitting and "doing nothing" with closed eyes can seem a bit frightening. But closing one's eyes and finding a place of stillness within is acknowledged by growing numbers of medical professionals to have many beneficial outcomes, such as lowering blood pressure, relieving tension, and reducing the risk of heart disease. In a state of quietude, subtle changes in consciousness are allowed to occur. While meditating, we become aware of a universe that is not readily apparent during normal daily activity.

The meditation we will use in this course is called the "Yin-Yang Light Meditation." Yin and Yang are the Chinese feminine and masculine cosmic principles, or the magnetic and dynamic forces of nature. One translation describes the dynamic Yang force as "flags flying in the sun," and the magnetic Yin force as "hidden in the dark mist." The Yang energy is embodied in the white light of the meditation. This is crystal clear white light, the bright light of the heavens. The Yin energy is dark violet light that bubbles up from the depths of the Earth, thick and rich like dark violet oil. This is the energy of the Great Mother.

This meditation is self-guided. It is based on the quantum principle that thought directs energy and energy follows thought. So, as you think of directing the light to flow through your body, the light follows your

THE POWER OF SELF-LOVE   39

thought. You don't have to visualize or force the light energy. It will move effortlessly where you direct it to go. When doing the meditation in your circle it works well if one woman actually guides the mediation verbally. (See "Suggestions For Weekly Meetings" in Appendix I.)

THE YIN–YANG ENERGY MEDITATION

To do the meditation, sit in a comfortable chair with both feet on the floor and your hands in your lap. Close your eyes. Take two or three deep breaths. As you release your breath, let any tension flow out of your body. As you return to your normal breathing pattern, sink into your chair and feel the Great Mother supporting you. Listen to your breath and feel its rhythm. Become aware that your breath is in harmony with all the rhythms of the planet—the winds, the tides, the seasons. Now, bring your focus to your third eye, which is a point in the middle of your forehead. With each breath, bring more and more of your awareness to this point, while simultaneously releasing all the worries of your daily life and allowing all of your attention to be focused in the moment.

Once you have focused your attention in your third eye, direct your awareness to an area about six to eight inches above your head. This is your eighth chakra. It is your transcendental chakra and is your connection to the entire physical and metaphysical universe. Inside this chakra is your own "Sacred Room." It is a place outside the normal everyday world where you can go anytime to relax and renew your spirit. It is a beautiful space that is completely your own.

Take a moment and just look around your Sacred Room. Relax and enjoy being there. You may find a comfy chair or a window seat where you might want to sit and read a book. You may want to open the door and go out into the garden, or down the path, through a forest, or onto the beach. The things you can do in your Sacred Room are boundless.

Now, go out of the door and walk down a path. Soon you see a young girl walking toward you. As she gets closer you realize that she is you as a young teenager around thirteen or fourteen. You are happy to see each other. You run into each other's arms and embrace. Feel yourself holding your teenage-self. Experience how happy this makes both of you. You begin to dance together. You tell her that the two of you are about to take a journey together. The excitement is palpable.

As you have been dancing together, a bright White Star has lighted and has begun filling the space around you with white light energy. You understand, as though you have known forever, that this is the white light of the cosmic Yang energy.

Now, direct the White Star to open and pour white light down from your Sacred Room into your head. Observe as the shower of bright white light pours down through your brain, your face, into your throat, down through all of your body, down through your arms and legs, and into your hands and feet.

When the light reaches your hands and feet, think of opening the palms of your hands and the bottoms of your feet and let the light wash into the Earth, carrying with it the psychic debris that has been picked up as it washed through your body. Become aware of subtle feelings and changes taking place in your body.

Next, think of moving with your thought down into a space about three feet below your feet. This is your Sacred Cave. Spend some time exploring your cave. This is the home of your Power Woman. After a few moments, your Power Woman emerges from the darkness. Allow her to embrace you. Feel the strength of her energy.

Now, a dark violet light appears. This energy is so dark it is almost black. This is the cosmic Yin energy. It is as powerful and as dark as the Great Mother herself. Direct this dark violet energy of the Great Mother to rise through the bottoms of your feet, up into your legs, up through your body, into your chest, down your arms, out the open palms of your hands. Continue directing the Yin energy up through your throat, into your face, and into your brain. As the dark violet light reaches the top of your head, direct your skull to open and allow the dark violet light to shoot up and out the top of your head. Then direct the dark violet light to wrap around your body like a great cape.

Now, focus back in your body as the dark violet Yin light moves up and the white Yang light moves down. Experience the white light and dark violet light energies swirling through your body and observe the feelings or sensations that may arise. Wherever you feel any pain or constriction, direct the light into that part of your body, intensify it, and allow it to do its healing work, melting away the obstructions or constrictions.

Float for a while in the light that is both filling you and surrounding you. Sink into the light. Let the light restore you, support you, and empower you. Become aware that you are nothing but light—a great powerful being of light. Stand in that powerful experience of your true-lighted self for a moment or two.

Now, move back into the Sacred Room above your head and direct the white light shower to stop. Next, move back down into your Sacred Cave and direct the dark violet light to stop. Close the bottoms of your feet, the palms of your hands, and the top of your head. Experience the lusciousness of your body filled with the light and dark energy.

Next, when you are doing this meditation with others, take this time to direct the light around the group clockwise to create a safe and sacred lighted circle. When you are doing the meditation alone, send the light around the Earth to bring healing and balance into our world.

Before opening your eyes, take a deep breath. Begin to wiggle your fingers and toes. Plant your feet solidly on the floor in front of you. Think of bringing all of your awareness into your feet to get grounded. Now, open your eyes slowly. Your re-entry should be gentle. Take a few moments to sit before moving into any activity. Stand and stretch. This helps the light to enter more areas of your body, and it feels good.

This meditation can be done in about ten minutes. As you become more adept you will expand to fifteen or twenty minutes. But ten minutes is perfectly fine for those just starting out.

By doing the meditation immediately after journaling, you will find that the light washes away and repairs much of the pain, discomfort, or anxiety that you may have uncovered as you were writing.

(**NOTE:** See Appendix II for a meditation outline sheet that you can refer to when you are first working with the meditation at home. It is also useful for those leading the meditation in the circle. Another way that you might find helpful in learning the meditation is to tape record your own voice reading the meditation and then follow along.)

DUTY VERSUS SELF–LOVE

Many of my students balk at the idea of having to do the journaling and meditation every day. They see engaging in their growth tools as a chore or a duty. Students often say to me, "I'm tired of doing what I'm supposed to do," or "I just felt like being good to myself today, so I didn't do my journaling or my meditation." I understand this attitude. There are so many things we are supposed to do and adding more to the list can sometimes feel overwhelming.

But this is where self-love enters.

Most of the things we are obliged to do in our lives are for others. They are also things that are part of the practical material world. Journaling and meditation are for no one but us. They are for our own personal growth and development. They connect us to our divinity. They can help you become all that you can be. The tools of journaling and meditation are for and about our spiritual lives; therefore, they exist outside of normal time. Though it may seem at first that you're sacrificing thirty to forty-five minutes a day by doing your journaling and meditation, as time goes on, you'll realize that the tools of your spiritual practice will actually create more time in your everyday life. I find that by doing this practice consistently it has become a soothing bridge between my sleep life and my awake life, which prepares me to slip into my day in a peaceful state of well being.

The acts of journaling and meditation are acts of self-love. Not doing them can actually be self-sabotage. You are a magnificent gemstone. Polishing that gemstone makes it shine. Journaling and meditation are your polishing cloths. You are reading this book and participating in this course in order to polish yourself to a high sheen, so that your light can shine throughout your life. A Power Woman does not neglect herself.

THE PRAYER

At the end of the day before we sleep, it is good to refocus our awareness on our Spirit. Prayer is a wonderful way to focus our attention and connect with the Divine Mother. You may say your own prayer or this one. In your circle it is always good to close with this prayer said out loud in unison.

The Woman's Prayer

Divine Mother,

As I step into this new era of my life, I am becoming more and more aware that you are with me, and that you express yourself through me.

When I open my heart to your great power, I feel you reminding me of how beautiful I am.

I feel you guiding me to embrace my creative talents.

I feel your support as I make a deeper commitment to my purpose.

I begin to experience all the abundance that you so amply supply, and I hear you reminding me that you will supply all that I will ever need.

I ask you to remind me each day that I must honor my soul with meditation and my body with exercise and healthful food.

When it seems too dark to see the light, I know that you are always guiding me.

I know that you are beside me when I stumble, as I attempt to step out into the world to express my own true feminine power.

Help me to move more and more into my heart and realize that judgment is not mine, and that arrogance will trip me up every time.

I welcome your powerful spirit into my life, as I endeavor to become the most loving and creative partner and leader that I can possibly be.

Freedom is my goal. Love is my path. Commitment is my promise.

I feel your love always, and I feel blessed to be a woman.

Blessed be.

GAMES AND EXERCISES

In addition to the two basic tools, journaling, and meditation, each week there are games and exercises to accomplish. Committing to do them is also part of your self-love program. The tools and the games have been created to bring you into better alignment with your higher self and your life's purpose.

Many of these games and exercises are oriented to the right brain and therefore work below your normal conscious awareness or left-brain understanding. Because of this, some of them may seem silly, or unnecessary. Our rational minds are wonderful things, but they have their place, and a large part of this course is directed at your less rational self, your newly ignited intuitive nature. All of the tools, games, and exercises are there for a reason. Some you will find fun, others will be challenging. Do them all.

At the beginning of each week read the list of games and exercises, so that you can plan ahead. You don't want to leave them until the last day, because they won't have time to cause the transformation for which they're designed.

GAMES AND EXERCISES

WEEK ONE: THE POWER OF SELF-LOVE

1. Journal daily. Write for 20 minutes (3 pages or more) first thing
    in the morning. Use an 8 1/2" x 11" ruled, spiral note pad.
    Remember to write without stopping and don't worry about
    the content or the punctuation.

2. Meditate daily. Immediately following your journaling, do the
    Yin-Yang Meditation for at least 10 minutes. Eventually you
    will work up to 20 minutes, but 10 minutes is good for the
    time being.

3. Write an affirmation that confirms your love for yourself each
    morning. Write it over and over at least 15 times. Then write it
    on a 3" x 5" card or any other small piece of paper and carry
    it with you all day. You may use the affirmations on page 35
    in this chapter, or make up your own.

4. Make a list of five songs from your teen years that made
    you feel strongly in any way.

5. Try to remember a favorite perfume or cologne from your
    . teen years. If it is still manufactured, buy some and wear it
    every day. (If it's a smell that you can't stand wearing
    nowadays, put some on a cloth and keep it near your face
    while you sleep.)

THE POWER OF

Creativity

"Living is a form of not being sure, not knowing what next or how.
The moment you know how, you begin to die a little.
The artist never entirely knows. We guess.
We may be wrong, but we take leap after leap in the dark."

– Agnes DeMille

S tanding on the foundation of self-love, our Power Women can now begin taking tiny steps toward creating a new life plan. You may perceive this as an exciting adventure, or a daunting challenge. But whatever feelings you have about your creativity, or your lack of it, as we begin to explore the Power to Create, keep in mind that we are all shaped in the likeness of a greater creator, making us all deeply creative beings.

This week we are going to ease into creativity. We are going to explore the simple creative things we did as children, when there was less riding on what we drew, painted or sculpted.

Many in our culture believe that creativity should be left to the artists, but who are artists and who is to judge? A woman in one of my circles had just returned from Bali when we began the course. She told the group that everywhere she went in Bali people were carving and painting beautiful masks. When she expressed her surprise to a Balinese man at the number of artists in such a small country, he laughed and said, "In Bali, everybody is an artist." In our society, where artists are considered a rarified breed, who live outside the normal bounds of society, this idea seems absurd

The very word creative is heavy with meaning; it reeks with potential. It harbors fear. It promises hope. According to Webster's: To create is "to bring into being. To give rise to. To produce through artistic or imaginative effort."

Women are natural-born creators. We come with a womb and all the other apparatus with which to birth babies. But when we arrive at the second half of our lives, that part of our creative potential is no longer available to us.

Part of the process of menopause is to grieve the loss of that creativity. We have lived since puberty for the biological purpose of creating progeny. Now that is ending, or has ended. Of course, not all women have given birth to babies by the time they reach menopause, and their grief process over the death of eggs never used can exacerbate feelings of loss and depression. Luckily for all of us, creating babies is not our only purpose. In the Power Woman stage of life, we are freed from that biology and ready to fulfill our soul's purpose. To do this, we must create a new life for ourselves, based not in biology or society's idea of what our lives should be, but on what our souls and that bright new spark of intuition in our brains are pushing us toward.

WOMEN AS CREATORS

In the prehistoric era of the hunter-gatherers, human beings thought only women were involved in the birth process. These ancient peoples witnessed human life coming from a mortal woman's womb, and therefore believed that all of life was born from the womb of the Divine Mother. The creativity of the feminine was revered. Not only did we create babies, but also a strong, hardy species called the human race. It wasn't until somewhere between five and ten thousand years ago that men realized their part in the conception of children. With this understanding of their role in procreation, men developed a new sense of their importance in the tribe. They were no longer merely hunters and supporters of the women who did the important work of creating life. Now they saw that they were part of the creative process, and they thus became possessive of their own offspring and the family lines that would give them immortality.

To ensure there would be no doubt of their lineage continuing, they not only claimed their children as property, but also their children's mothers. This change in the social structure engendered new spiritual practices. The Divine Mother gave way to multiple gods and goddesses. Whereas the Great Goddess had men as consorts, now male gods became equal to the female gods and by early in the third millennium BCE, the male gods gained higher status than the female gods. Slowly over time, in the Near East, Europe, and the Middle East, the pantheon of gods was superceded by one all-powerful male Abrahamic deity: known as Yahweh, God, and Allah. But the progression of human history would not exist without the ability of all humans to create more than mere replicas of ourselves.

Humanity has created societies, civilizations, science, and art. We have crossed oceans, mountain ranges, and traveled to the moon and beyond. Creativity is the very heart of our nature. And though men have been the ones credited with these monumental creations, it is only because they have —usually with the use of brute force—maintained the stronger voice. Women's accomplishments are written in a lighter hand, drawn on the walls of one-room schoolhouses, in the halls of hospitals, in the convents of the Middle Ages.

Women have not had a strong voice in the creation of society for more than five thousand years, but we have never been completely silenced. Now, at the beginning of a new millennium, it is time for women to recover our voices—to reconnect to the powerful creativity that led the human race steadily forward over the entire span of human existence. In the ancient cultures, the young women were busy with the babies. The grandmothers were responsible for creating the society in which the children could survive and grow into healthy adults.

Questions to Ponder

- *What does creativity mean to you?*
- *What do you do creatively in your daily life?*
- *Can you think of ten creative things you've done in your life? Try. Try harder.*

WHO GETS TO BE CREATIVE?

We hunger for creativity. As children we create constantly. We draw pictures, make papier-mâché toys, finger paint, make up characters, and play endlessly fascinating games. Then we grow up. Our lives fill with the practical and the mundane. Some of us are fortunate enough to have careers that call on our creative talents. But many of us aren't that lucky.

We feel that to be creative with abandon, the way we did as children, is self-indulgent. We live in a society that doesn't value creativity, so we suppress our desire to play make-believe or to smear globs of paint over a yard of butcher paper. Most of us are steeped in the belief systems of a society that says it's a waste of time to do silly creative stuff. Those celebrities who do make a living in the creative fields, do so on such a rarefied level that it seems ridiculous for the average person to even try. To consider oneself an actor, writer, painter, or musician in our culture, one must be paid huge amounts of money; therefore, most of us go through life thinking that we aren't creative.

We are all artists. We are all extremely creative. Most women, and even many men, love to make beauty in their homes and gardens. But it wasn't until Martha Stewart came along that the arts of the home were acknowledged in the broader society. Now, home decorating, crafts, and cooking monopolize cable television. And men are beginning to participate in them, too.

Questions to Ponder

- *Do you garden, cook, decorate your house?*
- *Do you think that these things are creative and artistic?*
- *Have you ever finished creating something and suddenly felt a surge of joy, like a song was about to burst from your heart?*
- *From where do you think creativity springs?*

THE FEAR OF CREATING

It's time to seek the creativity lurking just below the surface of our conscious awareness. It's time to allow it to bubble up and begin to inform our developing selves of our true creative potential. This week we're going to finger paint. Next week we will make collages, and the week after that we'll write poetry. These are games and exercises. They are not about creating professional art, but they will allow our creativity to toddle onto the stage.

If you're doing this course in a circle, you may feel badly that your projects don't seem to be as artistic or professional as some done by other women in the circle. Don't worry about it. The purpose is not about being good; **it's about being bold**. It's about crying out to the world and telling yourself, "I am a creative being, and I will create no matter what!"

And if you feel your creative efforts are better than some of your sisters', enjoy the beauty you have created, but drop the competition. We are sisters, who each bring our own magnificent piece to the mosaic of life.

A great deal of fear surfaces when we think about being creative. Fear is the emotion that blocks all good things in our lives. Fear is the dragon we must slay to become all that we can be.

One of the most important things about the second half of life is the gate that we go through to get there. That gate is menopause. Everyone is afraid of the unknown, and menopause still remains unfamiliar territory. Perhaps if our daughters watch us as we unveil the mystery and embrace the departure of the childbearing woman and the joy of being born into our Power Woman, they will enter menopause with less apprehension.

But I'm not convinced that menopause is supposed to be easy. There is a certain amount of the death/rebirth process that must remain a mysterious journey for each of us. Diving into the dark mystery is how we find the treasure.

In the previous chapter, we talked about the descent of Inanna into the underworld, where her sister Ereshkigal, the Goddess of Death, hanged her on a meat hook. There, her body rotted and eventually she was eaten by demons. As we continue our journey through this course, we will observe Inanna's eventual resurrection. But for now, we are interested in the creative juices that begin to simmer as we descend into the underworld. Here we find ourselves deprived of the old garments of the childbearing woman, stripped naked in the midst of an unknown world of darkness.

I spent three years in the depths of the underworld. But in the midst of pounding headaches, hot flashes, and bouts of depression, among other things, I created a garden. I lived in an apartment in Studio City, California. The front windows overlooked a swimming pool, but my back deck faced a driveway. Next to the driveway was an expanse of dirt about twenty feet deep and a hundred feet long that had been barren for years.

Each day I dug and planted that sterile patch of dirt. In three years, I had created an incredible garden complete with trees, a birdbath, a small patch of lawn, morning glories, bougainvillea, and a winding path that meandered through flowerbeds where zucchini, beans, basil, and pumpkins twined among the blooms. As I created this magnificent garden, I descended into darkness.

I remember one day in particular. The plants had grown tall by this time, so I was hidden from passersby as I pulled weeds and tilled the dirt with my hand trowel. As I dug up a piece of earth, my own death began to unfold before me. I felt as though my body was dying. It was as though life was flowing out of me and down into the earth. I thought of my body buried under the garden and the worms and spiders crawling over me as I lay rotting. I breathed this vision into my lungs, and I felt a deep, sensual, almost erotic thrill in the back of my throat. Then and there, I decided that when I died I wanted to be buried directly in the ground encased in nothing and wearing only a white cotton dress so that my body could decompose along with all other dead things and become one with the Mother Earth.

When I was finished with my gardening that day I went inside and told my husband about my experience, and how I wanted to be buried. Thankfully, he was compassionate and even interested. I consider this the most extraordinary day of my menopause. I had gone into the final level of the underworld. I had died, and each day after that was a step back up toward life on Earth. Like Inanna, I retrieved the garments of my life, one by one, at the seven gates of hell on my return.

The fact that during my "dying time" I created a beautiful, abundant, and radiant garden of living things is a metaphor for our lives as women in the second half of life. Our creativity is brought forth in a new way, a much more powerful and expressive way than ever before in our lives. Fear is the darkness where we descend and creativity is what we bring forth out of that darkness.

Questions to Ponder

- *If you believed you had the talent to make any kind of art in the world, what would you make?*
- *Did anyone ever tell you that you were a talented writer, artist, dancer, musician?*
- *Did anyone ever tell you that you didn't have any talent?*

THE CREATIVE CHILD BECOMES THE CREATIVE TEEN

As children we were wildly creative. We colored and painted daily. In Brownie Scouts and Bluebird Girl meetings we made crafts of every kind. Then just as we were beginning to develop some actual expertise in our artistic endeavors, we hit puberty. And with this onslaught of hormones everything in our lives changed dramatically. We became obsessed with the strangest things. We were growing breasts and buying brassieres. Boys, who had been simply bothersome, were suddenly interesting. Clothes and popularity became tantamount. But with all of this came a feeling of inse-curity. This new world and these new physical and emotional sensations introduced an extreme sense of imbalance. We were living on the brink of something, and we didn't know what it was.

We learned about our changing bodies from embarrassed mothers and stone-faced schoolteachers. Some of us got better preparation than others about our periods, but few girls were left with the impression that month-ly bleeding was a good thing.

I remember the summer that I got my first period. I was thirteen and working as an apprentice in a summer stock company. As a dresser for the leading ladies, I was like a fly on the wall in the crowded dressing room watching these goddesses of the New York stage as they sat in front of makeup mirrors in their underwear, smoking cigarettes, and talking in brassy tones about anything that popped into their minds—the show, their love affairs, other shows, and famous performers' sexy secrets.

One actress in particular, Mary McCarty, was louder, funnier, and bawdier than the others. I was her personal dresser for the week she played the lead in *Call Me Madam*. She was a little overweight, and the extra flesh spilled out of her black bra and girdle. Every night the producer would come into the dressing room, give her a big kiss on the cheek and wish her good luck. Then, in her low whiskey voice, she'd tell him what a darling he was and off he'd go.

But one night Mary brushed him aside with a dramatic flick of her wrist. "Stay away from me tonight, honey, I've got the *curse*, and I don't give a damn about you or your show!" And she slapped him on the behind. He backed out of the dressing room, hopelessly trying to maintain a sense of dignity, while Mary and the other actresses roared with laughter.

There I was, a thirteen-year-old from a conservative, middle-class home, standing in the corner watching this amazing exchange. I was giddy with an overwhelming feeling of forbidden excitement. At the same time, I was horribly embarrassed that this actress had spoken of the *secret woman's thing* to a man.

Looking back on that moment from a distance of forty-some years, I realize how much there is to be mined from such a potent memory. The complex feelings, thoughts, and lasting impressions are powerful inscriptions in my psyche.

In 1958, girls from nice little suburban homes didn't see bold women like this in such an intimate setting. Just the idea of a man being in the same room with a woman in her underclothes who wasn't his wife was unthinkable. Women rarely, if ever, spoke to men with such disregard, especially if they worked for them, and they NEVER, EVER mentioned their periods to men.

This entire event was tremendously empowering. Looking back on it, I realize it was like being in a sanctuary of outrageous, creative women. It was the closest a '50s American girl would ever come to being in a red tent or moon hut. Yet, buried in the center of this experience lies one crippling phrase—"I've got the *curse.*" A powerful woman, demeaning her own femininity.

The very next week I got my first period. My only preparation for this most holy of female passages had been a quick, chagrinned description of menstruation and the use of Kotex belts and pads from my mother, bleak stick figures and black-and-white drawings of ovaries and fallopian tubes from a grade-school health film, and that very descriptive phrase, filled with loathing, from a woman I admired and dreamed of emulating. For years I called my period the *curse.* It was powerful. In my mind it was directly connected to a woman's ability to have power over men, to *curse* them and make it stick. The vision of that producer backing out of the room, completely flummoxed by a woman with the *curse* was deeply satisfying.

But at school things were quite different. I wanted to be an actress. I had played at acting as a child, but as a young teen I wanted to perfect it.

I wanted to become a real actress. I wanted to excel, to succeed. I was a potent female with a lot of talent. And there was no place for that at California Junior High School. The auditions for plays became popularity contests, which the teachers were unwittingly, or wittingly, drawn into. Girls who actively pursued making a name for themselves in artistic or creative ways were shunned, considered art geeks. My mother told me again and again, "Don't let them know you care! Don't be so bold, it frightens people." And sadly, over time, I learned that she was right.

But almost all girls deal with the same kinds of insecurities and negation of their creative spirits, whether they balk as I did or shut down and knuckle under the expectations of their parents and society. In the '50s and early '60s, we were expected to wear white gloves, attend teas and talk nearly exclusively about boys. In the late '60s and through the '70s, society had loosened up a bit, but although we saw creative women emerging on television, society in general still expected young women to focus their creative potential on finding a husband and settling down.

Society taught us to drop our creative yearnings and focus on the competition. We learned to see our girlfriends not as sisters suffering the same fate as ourselves, but as competitors for the same popular boys. Instead of developing our talents, we developed our abilities to coyly attract boys, acquire letter sweaters, and become good girlfriends. Grades and studying came only after boys, cliques, and clubs. Artistic endeavors and creative desires for most of the girls I knew were almost completely suppressed. And those who did excel in creative activities such as music, art, or theatre did so at the expense of their popularity and their dating lives.

First periods are like last periods. They mark a biological change in our bodies. With each, we are on the brink of new life. Creativity is the very essence of new life. And at the beginning of new life we feel a sense of imbalance and insecurity. We search for clues from the past. In menopause we are fortunate to be able to look back at our adolescence. The only trick is to remember it. Some of those suppressed dreams and desires and the way in which we buried them lie hidden in a pretty thick fog. But with a little prodding we can clear away the haze.

Questions to Ponder

- *What do you remember about the events surrounding your first period?*
- *Who did you want to be like when you grew up?*
- *What are some of the creative things you wanted to do when you were a teenager? How many of them did you do in your life?*
- *As a teenager, did you talk about your dreams and desires with your girl-friends? Your parents? Your boyfriends?*

WOMEN IN CIRCLES CREATING THEIR NEW LIVES

The fact that as teenagers we had few girlfriends with whom we truly felt safe makes it difficult for women, even in the second half of life, to be completely supportive of one another. Although many of us wish for and believe in loving our sisters, it is a lesson that is hard to embrace fully. This comes from our long history of having to compete for men. Until the twentieth century, women couldn't live in this world without the help of a man or men. If a woman wasn't married, she usually had to be supported and housed by a male relative. Few women were able to make a living for themselves and create their own homes. This made getting a man and keeping him as much a survival issue as a love issue. Because of this, until recently, women couldn't trust women outside of their immediate families.

I lived in Italy in 1985, when women in the United States had broken through many patriarchal barriers. But in Italy I found it nearly impossible to make friends with Italian women. I worked with several wonderful women. They were making headway in their careers, but they were still steeped in the old way of women's relationships. Gina was thirty, beautiful, brilliant, and working as a production manager on films. She yearned for a group of girlfriends, but she couldn't trust women other than her close relations—her sisters, cousins and aunts. In her mind, all women were rivals who were out to steal her man. Ironically, her man was the husband of another woman.

Kelly is an American woman who married an Italian man and moved to Italy at twenty-two. When I met her, she had lived in Rome for twenty-five years and had just sent her last child off to college. She and her husband had split a couple of years before and she was seeing a new man, but she told me that when she looked around at her life, she realized how terribly lonely she was. All those years she'd only had her husband's mother, aunts, and sisters for companionship. Suddenly she realized she was hungry for women friends.

Kelly and I met another American woman and the three of us spent a good deal of time together that summer, taking walks in the park, having meals together, and talking about our hopes and dreams for the future. We were all in our forties and beginning to feel the call of our Power Women. Six months after I returned to the States, Kelly appeared on my doorstep. She had left her boyfriend, and when she considered what she wanted to do next, all she could think about was how happy she'd been that summer just hanging with girlfriends. She realized it was time to come home and make some lasting friendships.

The last time I saw her she had opened a gourmet food shop in West Los Angeles and had a woman's group that met there once a week. She said she had never been happier in her life, though she is still single. She still travels to Italy several times a year to visit her grown children, but not to stay. Her circle of women friends feeds her soul.

Power Women need to be part of a sisterhood. In our bonding as sisters we find our true individual power. Women, when not superficially acting as enemies for survival, are natural allies. And as allies we can help each other find our callings and unveil our unique creative geniuses. We can become each other's mentors.

Questions to Ponder

• *Has anyone ever been a mentor for you and your creativity?*
• *Would you like to have a creative mentor?*
• *Describe your ideal creative mentor.*

TIME TO CREATE

On her fiftieth birthday, the actress Meryl Streep said, "All I want is more time, and nobody can give me that all wrapped up with ribbon." We all want more time. We live in a world in which time has become a great luxury.

Yet I wonder what she meant exactly. Did she mean she wanted to have a longer time to live? Did she see turning fifty as a signal that time *is running out?* Or did she mean she just wanted more time in her daily life for the things that are truly important? She may have meant all of it. All are significant.

What we realize when we reach the mid-point in life is that there is an end. Until our mid-forties, we're pretty sure that only old people get old. Suddenly, it occurs to us that we will get old, too. At first this thought causes panic. But living in a constant state of panic is extremely uncomfortable. Slowly, over time, we become more philosophical about the inevitable end of life, which is a good thing. But we also have to keep remembering and acknowledging that the mid-point is the mid-point and not the end-point. Though we are constantly bumping up against society's expectations of menopausal and post-menopausal women, we must just as insistently reaffirm that we are or are becoming Power Women now, and are not yet Crones. We probably have as many years in the second half of life as we had in the first half, and our Power Woman stage will continue for as long as we remain healthy, active, and interested in pursuing our dreams and accomplishing our work.

The fact is that we do have time—plenty of time to start a new career, create a new lifestyle, learn a new instrument, begin a new spiritual discipline, or find a new life partner. You may not choose to become the ballet dancer you dreamed of in your youth, but you may become an interpretive dancer, study dance, write about dance, or just go out dancing once a week. You may not settle down with a life partner with the intention of raising children, but you may find a loving partner with whom you can create a business, write books together, or just enjoy sharing life. In the Power Woman stage, our creative endeavors become our children.

If we look at the other possible meaning of Meryl Streep's quote—that she wants more time in her daily life—then we can allay that fear by looking at the magical stretching of time. Time is malleable. It is all in how we perceive it. If we meditate every day, our time will begin to stretch, because we are spending some part of each day outside of time. This causes a crack in our perception of time. We will begin to see ourselves with much more time for the things we love to do. We will begin dropping the false responsibilities we have taken on over the course of our lives and become willing to allow the true responsibilities to enter. We'll develop discernment and make friends with people who contribute positively to our lives, and we'll let those people who drain our energy fall by the wayside.

One wonderful thing about knowing there is an end, and that we are in the second half of life, is that we begin to value time much more. And in the valuing of time we begin to spend it wisely, and stretch it lovingly.

ROLE MODELS TO EMULATE

When we begin to explore the possibilities for the second half of our lives and the Power Women we are becoming, we naturally look for role models to emulate. And although the list of famous, mature women in history is not as long as that of men, there are still many commanding historical and contemporary women to whom we can look for guidance. We can also look around us for role models in our own families or communities.

I remember with awe a woman from my childhood whom everyone called "Grandma Dixon." She lived in a large old Victorian house in my hometown of Sacramento, California. She was not my grandmother, nor was she the grandmother of anyone I knew. But everyone wanted to claim relation to her.

Her home was the center for gatherings for several hundred people, who showed up at different times for Sunday dinner, weekday afternoon tea, or Christmas Eve. I was just six years old when she died at the age of 97, so my memory of her is sketchy. I do remember playing with other children in her garden, while the adults sat with Grandma Dixon and listened to her tell stories. Her house sat on a tree-lined residential street but it had originally been the main house of a large ranch where she grew up in the late nineteenth century. Her family had come from somewhere in the south after the Civil War.

One day I remember coming in from the back yard and climbing on my mother's lap. I couldn't have been more than three or four. Grandma Dixon was telling a story. I only remember little bits of the tale, but in it Grandma Dixon was a young girl, and she and her mother were alone on the ranch when some wild horses broke down the corral fence and some of the prize horses escaped. Grandma Dixon and her mother gave long, hard chase on horse back and at last rounded up the horses and returned them to the ranch.

The picture of that chase across the Sacramento Valley and the electricity of the moment when Grandma Dixon told the story to that small group in her parlor on Curtis Way are etched firmly in my memory. I had no living grandparents, so Grandma Dixon was my only powerful mature feminine role model. My mother was raised by homesteaders in the far northern reaches of California, and it was the tough pioneer life that killed her mother when she was very young. Grandma Dixon must have been an important figure in my mother's orphaned life. Something I never realized until writing this.

I would love to know Grandma Dixon's entire story. Unfortunately, she and all who knew her died long ago. But I can find tales of other strong pioneer women, and reading them, I get a better sense of what Grandma Dixon's life was like.

When we begin to create our Power Woman lives, we need role models. Women like Grandma Dixon can help us realize our potential.

In this chapter's "Games and Exercises" we will look for Power Woman role models, choose a role model, research her life over the course of the next six weeks and write a brief report about her accomplishments. You may have a powerful grandmother or other woman in your own family or acquaintance. If so, you may choose to study her life and learn what experiences, choices, and challenges led her to become a powerful woman in the second half of her life. Or you can look for role models in famous women of the past or present, such as Eleanor Roosevelt, Gloria Steinem, Oprah Winfrey, Helen Keller, Maya Angelou, Barbara Jordan, Bella Abzug, Eleanor of Acquataine, Georgia O'Keeffe, Hildegarde of Bingen.

These are just a few of the formidable women who made a difference in their middle and later years, and who may enlighten and inspire you. But don't limit yourself to the women on this short list. Explore. Find the Power Woman role model that is just the right fit for you.

Perhaps your role model is an African-American woman such as Sojourner Truth. Born a slave in New York at the end of the eighteenth century, she escaped from her master, became a minister, preached the gospel of freedom, and helped hundreds of freed slaves find new lives after the Civil War. Or Harriet Tubman, a runaway slave who led more than three hundred others to freedom as a conductor of the "underground railroad," and spent her later years lecturing against slavery, and for women's suffrage. Or Ida B. Wells, a late nineteenth- and early twentieth-century journalist, who advocated racial justice and women's rights. The Civil Rights movement of the 1950s and '60s gave us Rosa Parks, the first African American to refuse to sit at the back of the bus.

Important leaders in the Women's Suffrage movement of the nineteenth and early twentieth centuries include Elizabeth Cady Stanton, Susan B. Anthony, Lucretia Mott, and Jane Hunt. And before them was Mary Wollstonecraft, who in 1792 published the first great feminist treatise, *A Vindication of the Rights of Woman*. There are hundreds more in all eras and cultures.

Go to www.distinguishedwomen.com on the Web to find good lists of women and their accomplishments. This Web site also has a comprehensive list of books about distinguished women. Who can you think of?

As you delve into the life of your Power Woman role model, allow yourself to imagine yourself living a life like hers. Look at her life's challenges for similarities with your own. Think about ways large or small that you can make a difference in your community. Let your role model become one of your partners in this course.

Approach your role model as a teacher of creativity. Ask how you can become more creative, too. You are a creative being. What do you want to create next in your life?

G A M E S   A N D   E X E R C I S E S

WEEK TWO: THE POWER OF CREATIVITY

1. This is an ongoing exercise for the next six weeks. Choose your
    Power Woman role model. Research her life by reading books,
    gathering biographical material on the Internet, and any other
    sources you can find. Your Power Woman role model must be
    a woman who in her Power Woman stage of life made or is
    making a positive difference in her community, her country, or
    the world. You may choose from women currently in the
    public eye, women in history, or even women in your family,
    an ancestor perhaps, as well as someone you know. The most
    important requirement is that you admire the woman.

    The second requirement is that she has a life that can be
    researched in some depth. At the end of six weeks you will be
    asked to share the essence of what you have learned about
    your Power Woman role model by giving a brief report to
    your circle. If you are doing this course alone, you may want
    to write up an article about your role model to send to your
    local paper or create a Web site about her so you can share
    the information with others.

    (**NOTE:** During the circle meetings of weeks eight, nine, and
    ten, you will want to set aside time for the role model reports.
    These reports should be no more than five to six minutes long,
    and depending on the size of your circle, you can have two,
    three, or four women report each of these weeks.)

2. Go to a hobby shop or art supply store and buy finger paints
    and some butcher paper. Dress in your rattiest clothes.
    Turn on some music, perhaps some of your favorite songs
    from last week's games.

    Spread the butcher paper in an area that can be cleaned easily,
    dip your hands into the paint, and go at it. Make as many
    paintings as you want. Remember that finger painting is about
    expressing from your body. Your hands are part of your
    body. Don't think about what you're going to paint. Just paint.

3. Find one picture of yourself between the ages of 13 and 18.
    Make or buy a frame for it. Put it on your dresser and look
    at it every morning and every evening.

4. Paint your fingernails and toenails a wild color. Wear it for a
    week. (**NOTE:** This is a game that you could do in your circle.
    Each person can bring a bottle of polish. Pair off and paint
    each other's toenails.)

5. Make a list of five articles of clothing and/or pieces of jewelry
    that you owned when you were a teen.

6. Make a list of three actresses you wanted to be like when you
    were a teen. See if you can discover where they are now?

REMEMBER to continue your journaling and meditation daily.
If you've missed a day, don't be angry with yourself, just get back
to it. The more you journal and meditate, the more powerful these
tools become.

THE POWER OF

Self-Trust

*"You were born God's original.
Don't try to become someone's copy."*

– Marian Wright Edelman

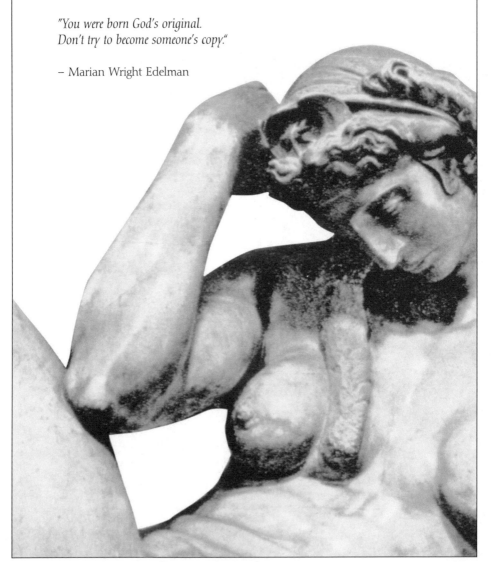

As we set out to create a new life, we must be able to trust our instincts and be ready to follow our hearts. Our Power Woman is not someone who blindly follows the lead of others. She must stand for her own beliefs and values. To trust ourselves, we must know ourselves. As we move through the Eleven Points of Power, we are adding to that knowledge every day. Self-knowledge is the key to self-trust.

To embrace self-trust, we must first take a look at self-doubt. Self-doubt is easy. We are all adept at it. By the time we reach midlife we have accumulated enormous experience with self-doubt. And the amazing thing is, we're often proud of it. We feel constantly driven to get another opinion. We Baby Boomer women buy more magazines and self-help books, and watch and listen to more TV and radio talk shows than any other demographic group in the country. We are constantly trying to find someone to advise us. We honestly believe that everyone else has a much better grasp of any situation than we do. For the most part, this stems from the amount of fear we embody around making our own decisions.

The fact is that we do know how to make decisions. This becomes obvious when we take stock of our lives. If we look back on all the times we were forced by circumstance to make decisions, we will see that the majority of these decisions were the right ones. Time gives us perspective. And perspective is knowledge, which in turn gives us confidence, if we let it.

Lack of self-trust is often amplified by certain social situations. We may feel embarrassed in large groups, shy around new people, or nervous before going to, or giving, a party. Some people become physically ill when confronted with giving a dinner party. One woman I know throws up before she has to speak in front of a group, and it's something she has to do often. People deal with uncomfortable social situations in different ways. Some people simply retreat and refuse to participate. Others become gregarious to a fault. Still others turn to alcohol—a couple of glasses of wine and the evening becomes manageable. All these feelings and our reactions to them come from lack of self-trust. We don't trust that we are good enough, powerful enough, beautiful enough, rich enough, witty enough, intelligent enough.

Thus it would seem that our lack of self-trust comes from being judged as unworthy by others. And initially it did stem from that. As adolescent women we were treated as though we were second-class citizens. We were molded in those painful post-pubescent years by a judgmental society that, more often than not, deemed us undeserving of respect. And when the budding woman is not respected she has no way to develop self-respect. With no self-respect there can be no self-trust, because we cannot trust what we don't respect.

Eating disorders are among the most horrific examples of lack of self-trust. Anorexia is a disease that has been created by the media, which teaches women to hate their bodies and become thin no matter what the cost. Many young girls, even pre-teens, who are afflicted with anorexia have a twisted belief that by refusing to eat, or by binging and purging, they are taking control of their lives, and standing up for themselves. We have been exposed to these thinner-than-life role models since the early 1960s. The British model Twiggy started it all with the Mod Generation. And the tragedy has gotten worse over the years. In 1983, Karen Carpenter died of a heart attack precipitated by anorexia. And recently, Mary-Kate Olsen of the Olsen twins was added to the long list of anorexic celebrities when, at eighteen, she required medical attention. Young women today travel to "pro-ana" (pro-anorexic) Web sites to find encouragement and community. These Web sites encourage young girls to take charge of their lives by starving themselves, in some cases, literally to death. Can there be any better example of lack of self-trust than not even trusting the basic instinct to feed oneself?

Yes, it's hard to trust ourselves in a society that values women so little. A society that is obsessed with "make-over madness." But as women in the second half of life who are preparing to become Power Women, we have a responsibility to learn to trust ourselves, so that we can be an example to the young girls and women coming behind us. So that we can help create a world in which girls' and women's bodies, minds, and souls are revered. So that to gain control over their lives, young women can learn to trust their instincts based on their own self-knowledge and self-worth.

Judith, an acting coach in Los Angeles, told me about a time when she was in her thirties. She'd been married and divorced twice and had recently broken up with a man who was quite a bit younger. The end of that particular relationship had been devastating, and she was in the process of healing from it when her best friend gave her a book called Smart Women, Stupid Choices.

Her first reaction was to feel grateful for having her intelligence acknowledged. "But," she told me, "as soon as I let go of the momentary ego stroke, I realized that rather than an affirmation of who I was, this book, or at least its title, was a criticism of how I had chosen to live my life."

She thought about the men she'd loved. None of her three major relationships had been easy. The breakups had been painful but the growth she'd made because of these relationships was immense. Each one of these men had brought her an enormous gift of life's challenges and life's joys.

"If I hadn't been with these remarkable men, I could never have become the woman I am today." When I asked her who she felt she was today, she replied, "A mother, a teacher, and a seeker. Each husband helped me learn those parts of myself. Being in relationship with these men also taught me to take what I needed and move on, to leave a situation when I wasn't being respected; and most importantly, to listen to my inner voice, and trust my own needs." She made those choices and trusted herself enough to enter into those relationships. "I wasn't a woman who made stupid choices. I was, and am, a woman who makes choices and takes risks as they present themselves."

And from these choices, these decisions, these risks, Judith continues to mine precious gems of wisdom and to find more and more of her own true self.

Thanks to this lack of self-trust, most of us have spent the first half of our adult lives turning to others for guidance. We ask our family, our friends, strangers on Web sites and the media to tell us what is wrong with us, how to improve our appearance, lose weight, wear make-up, buy clothes, have sex, find jobs, attract husbands, and raise children.

Now, with years of life experience behind us, it's time to stop listening to others. It's time to relinquish our dependence on other people's opinions and to trust our own knowledge and instinct.

Questions to Ponder

- *Do you trust yourself?*
- *Do you think you trust others more than you trust yourself?*
- *Do you find yourself checking for a second, third, or fourth opinion before making major or even minor decisions? Does this help?*
- *Have you made choices in your life that you think are stupid? Can you find a way to see them as gifts?*

HIDE, SHOUT, OR ORDER

Until we learn self-trust, we all have different ways of dealing with challenging situations. Some of us tend to behave like turtles retreating into our shells when our world seems to whirl out of control. Others become like the Cowardly Lion and make lots of superfluous noise, stomping about, trying to frighten the enemy with silly postures. Still others transform into little tin soldiers, ordering everyone about while trying desperately to get things under control.

These categories aren't exclusive. Depending on the situation, we might practice one or another or combinations of all three behaviors. We may hate confrontations and find ourselves becoming the turtle in some circumstances.

Righteous indignation triggers the Cowardly Lion, who roars ineffectually, then retreats. Sometimes there is a closet turtle hiding within a tin soldier. We may be so afraid to stand up for what we believe to be necessary or right, that we create a rigid personality demanding strict adherence to specific rules, so that order can be maintained.

None of these ways of dealing with life's challenges works. We may have fooled ourselves into believing that they do, but if we are honest with ourselves, we know that such coping mechanisms have yielded few if any positive results.

When we hide, no one knows what we want. We simply waste our lives inside shells that may spare us from confrontation, but also keep us from achieving our goals. If we bluster and roar, we are perceived as fools and therefore lack the respect necessary for success. And if we try to strictly control every situation, we make enemies and find ourselves with fewer and fewer friends and little left to control.

Questions to Ponder

- *Do you react to certain situations by being a turtle, a Cowardly Lion, and/or a tin soldier?*
- *Do you have other ways of reacting ineffectually to challenging situations?*
- *Do you know anyone who exudes self-trust? If so, what might you do to emulate that person?*

Sally is an investment banker. She has a commanding presence in any crowd, but when she talks about her relationship with her son, she suddenly becomes the Cowardly Lion.

"*I raised Josh alone from the time he was eleven. His father was in the same town, but they only saw each other every other weekend. By the time he was fifteen he was quite a bit taller than I, and this seemed to give him a new sense of power. When I had exhausted my repertoire of what I considered rational approaches to getting him to do whatever it was I wanted done, I'd plant myself in front of this six-foot, gangly boy-monster, point my finger with firm resolve, and shake it toward his chin. Then I would proceed to yell as loud as I could. Each time I did this I was sure that it would accomplish whatever end I was pursuing at the time. But it never did. In fact, instead of scaring him, it made him laugh.*"

Sally couldn't figure out why he wouldn't take her seriously, because when his father told him the very same thing he would obey.

"*Since his father and I were divorced, I didn't get to observe him in action often, but when I did, I was always impressed at how easily he was able to get Josh's attention. He didn't scream or threaten, he just told him what he expected. The next time I needed to discipline Josh, I would think back to how his father had handled the previous situation, and I would imitate it. I would say the same words. I would use the same tone of voice, but it never worked.*"

What Josh's father had that Sally lacked was complete faith that what he said would be heard and obeyed. He didn't have to pretend to be strong, loud, or effectual, because he was. He trusted himself. Even though Sally was a woman who commanded authority in the work world, she wasn't able to do the same at home.

WHO INVENTED FIRE?

For the past five thousand years, the majority of the world's cultures have been functioning in what Rianne Eisler, in *The Chalice and the Blade*, calls a "dominator model." This is a society that depends on dominators and dominated. According to Eisler, before this dominator model, we practiced a partnership model, in which people worked together for the good of the whole. Instead of chieftains or kings, partnership societies had councils. Men and women were equals and everyone had a voice. War was unheard of and preserving life was of the utmost importance. In this pre-dominator era, the Great Goddess was the Mother of all.

With the development of the dominator model, war and winning dominance over others came to define the new paradigm. Women who had been revered, now became chattel to be won and possessed by men. Until this time, personal ownership was almost non-existent. In this new model, one had to own things to show power. Women, who by their very nature threatened this new way of life, had to be subjugated. This wasn't an easy task. Women and feminine principles were a potent force. It took three or four millennia for the new dominator model to achieve complete dominance.

As women became the property of men, they were taken from their mother's homes and given to the husband's family, thus breaking the strong bond of the mother-daughter relationship. Women's monthly lunar meditations in the "red tent" or the "bleeding hut" became illegal, therefore separating women during their most potent time. Women were, for the first time in history, dependent upon strong dominator men for their survival. A woman without a man lived outside of society. She had no way to make a living in this new society, unless she became a prostitute, and men made laws forbidding that profession even as they patronized it.

Suddenly, women who had been loving sisters became rivals, competing for men to take care of them. Women were taught to hate and distrust their sisters based on the same strategy that the Roman armies used to take over the world: divide and conquer.

With the coming of Christianity, the final segregation of women was sealed. From that point, two distinct social definitions of women emerged:

the Virgin and the Magdalene. Interestingly, both were named Mary, a word derived from *mare*, which means sea in all Romance languages, as well as several others. It is also one of the most ancient words for mother.

With this division firmly established, the war between the virgin and the whore raged for two thousand years, keeping women estranged and therefore powerless. Men had the best of both Marys, keeping one as mistress and one as wife and mother of his children. In Europe, this way of life continues, accepted, even today.

Thus it came to be believed the Virgin and the Magdalene were natural enemies. This suited the dominators' purposes perfectly, for as long as women fought each other, distrusted each other, and hated each other, they posed no threat. Historically, men's greatest fear has been that women would unite.

As we work together in our circles, we are reclaiming the potency of the pre-dominator era. We are taking back our power. We are exercising our right to gather as women. Since the sexual revolution of the '60s and '70s, the division between women has weakened considerably. The woman who sleeps around and the good wife aren't necessarily two separate people anymore. The line between the virgin and the whore has softened, as has the line between the woman who speaks her mind and the one who minds her manners. A woman doesn't have to be one or the other. We have been split down the middle both as a sex and as individual women for two thousand years. We are now integrating all the parts of ourselves, and we love it.

In the pre-dominator Paleolithic and Neolithic eras, there is little evidence to suggest that human beings engaged in war. Weapons of war are rarely found in Neolithic archaeological sites. Though scientists have led us to believe that dominance by an alpha-male is the Homo sapiens' prototype, this assumption is finally being questioned. Until recently, it was assumed that the chimpanzee, an alpha-male dominated species, was our closest primate relative. The discovery of another primate species, the bonobo, shows it, in fact, to be our closest primate relative, sharing 98 percent of the same genes with humans. The bonobos, who live in The

Democratic Republic of the Congo (Zaire), maintain a non-violent society in which the female principles of nurturing and community are its mainstays. There are no alpha-males among the bonobos. And they work out their frustrations and differences by having sex, which they do exuberantly many times a day.

At the dawn of the new millennium, a brand new picture of women and feminine principles is unfolding. As we learn more about our prehistoric female ancestors, our own self-esteem can be enhanced.

Recently, while imagining our prehistoric mothers and grandmothers, it occurred to me that it must have been an older woman who brought fire to the tribe. I remember a drawing in my grammar-school history book of a hairy man rubbing sticks together and making the first fire. But what we know now of the Paleolithic era, suggests a much different scene. Men were the hunters. They left the cave and went on long hunting trips that lasted days and even weeks. The women stayed close to the cave. They foraged for berries and healing herbs, fed the babies, cared for the sick, and prepared the meat when the men returned. They ate the meat raw, because fire had not been discovered.

In this era the main focus was on survival. And the women's foremost concern was to give birth and keep the babies alive.

Imagine yourself as a grandmother in a Paleolithic tribe. You have learned a great deal about herbal remedies and food preparation. Over your long life, perhaps forty years, you have prayed to the Great Mother and have become adept at reading the signs she gives you.

It is a bitter cold day. Two of the babies are struggling to stay alive. You are not tied down to the cave by nursing and mothering duties, so you go out to gather herbs, hoping to find a remedy for the babies' illness.

A storm comes up. Lightning strikes a tree very close to you and causes it to burst into flame. You have seen this happen in the past, but never before have you been so close to the fire. It frightens you, but before you run, you realize that the fire is warm. You think of the cold, sick babies. It occurs to you that babies die more often in the cold part of the year than in the summer. You put two and two together. This warm fire might help the babies live. You're afraid of the fire, but you are also a woman. You know how important it is to keep the children alive. So, driven by your instincts for the survival of your brood, you pick up a piece of dry wood and stick it into the fire. It lights. Amazed and scared, you hurry back to the cave with this possible cure for the children. You make a pile of sticks and create a bigger fire. The sick children huddle around the fire. They live through the night.

There seems little doubt that older women, the grandmothers, made most of the major discoveries of the pre-historic era. We are the nurturers and healers of an entire species. Men were busy hunting. They had no time for anything else. Naturally, they invented and developed hunting weapons, but other innovations, such as fire, pottery, cooking, basketry, weaving, farming, healing, more likely than not came under the auspices of the women.

People did not engage in war, for during the Paleolithic era there weren't enough humans to waste life so unnecessarily. They banded together in partnership, helping each other survive. Unity, community, nurturing, survival of the race—these are all feminine aspects of humanity. This is our heritage. This is the deep memory we women must reconnect with, so that we can begin to remember just how powerful we are.

PUBERTY AND HISTORY

When we begin to menstruate, a flash of cellular memory is activated reminding us of the extraordinary part we played in the birth and survival of our species. Because we are no longer prepared for our transition into womanhood, nor trained, as we once were, to listen to the messages from our bodies, we have no context in which to place this extraordinary event. But if we look carefully at young girls entering puberty we can get a sense of it. There is a brash, confident, even outlandish air about them. The look in their eyes says they know something powerful, dark, something of life and death. Often this look is mischievous, and very often it can seem threatening, when we don't know where it comes from or what it means.

In Neolithic times, this flash of cellular memory was probably understood by the grandmothers and revered. Most likely it was acknowledged and honored in the young women's menses celebrations. But today that look is misread. Misunderstood. Feared. It is considered dangerous in our male dominated world. It holds the hint of a sexuality that can't be controlled. It is squelched as fast as it appears.

This is the moment we must recover. This is where we will find the audacity to trust ourselves.

Questions to Ponder

- *Is there someone in your life right now whom you trust?*
- *Who have you trusted in the past?*
- *Have you ever trusted someone who betrayed your trust? Who? How did that betrayal affect you?*

SELF–TRUST AND OUR SPIRIT

We have been raised in a society that has cut itself off from a divine source. We feel at loose ends with no one to whom we can turn for help and guidance. The "one male god" of our culture hasn't necessarily given women much succor, and for the most part, Western society has made science our god.

But women naturally yearn for a connection with a Divine source. And when we become aware that we truly are connected to a Divine Spirit, we can relax a little and see that self-trust is part of trusting in Spirit, our own Spirit in conjunction with a Divine Spirit.

To become aware of your Divine connection to Spirit, think back on your life until you remember an experience you had entailing some form of guidance or help, which came from a place outside the realm of logic. Everyone has these kinds of events in their lives. We often refer to them as miracles. Carl Jung speaks of them as synchronicities.

The best times to search for these irrational, divine moments are during the rough periods in your life. The most difficult of life's circumstances
—when we can't control the situation, fix the hurt, or solve the problem—
often force us to surrender to the Divine, because we simply don't have
the strength to handle some things on our own. Death, divorce, severe
accidents, and money losses are a few of the things that can trigger a
Divine intervention.

The responsibility of raising a child can often be overwhelming, especially for very young mothers. There you were, footloose and fancy free, and
suddenly the life of this tiny person is given into your care. You know it is
your responsibility to keep this baby safe, but the world is a frightening
place, and some days it seems like you may not be able to protect your child.

At twenty-two, I had an eighteen-month-old son. I lived in a constant
state of fear that he would hurt himself and die. One day I took him to the
beach for the first time. It was a gorgeous Southern California day. I set my
precious baby boy down on a blanket and sat back to watch him experience the beauty of the ocean. The first thing he did was toddle off the blanket and scoop a handful of sand into his mouth. I leapt up and cleaned the
sand out of his mouth the best I could and scolded him. Within seconds
he was right back at it. I was very upset. I wasn't sure what eating sand
would do, but I knew it couldn't be good. Nothing I did or said made the
slightest impression on him. I took him into the water to play in the waves,
but he just scooped up the wet sand and ate that.

I was becoming exhausted. The only thing I could think to do was take
him home, but we were with other people who weren't ready to leave.
Then, for no apparent reason, I was enveloped with an overwhelming calm.
I sensed that I should stop worrying—that my baby would be all right. The
knowledge that his life wasn't in my hands popped into my mind like a little epiphany. Someone, somewhere was telling me that the life and death of
my child was out of my control. From that moment, I became a more
relaxed mother. I learned to let him try things and find out for himself,
when it was appropriate. I didn't relinquish my responsibility, but I realized
that I wasn't alone. I began to trust that I was doing the very best job I

could, and that the rest was not up to me. I have been reminded many times since that I am not alone. And each time I let go to trust Divine Spirit, I am able to trust myself a little more at the same time.

Questions to Ponder

- *Can you remember a time when you trusted your own judgment completely?*
- *Can you remember a time when you knew a Divine power was helping or guiding you?*
- *Have you ever had to give up and just trust that your life or the situation was out of your hands?*

AFFIRMATIONS

- *I trust my instincts.*
- *I listen to my inner voice.*
- *I trust that I can make good decisions.*
- *I trust in myself more than others.*
- *I am trustworthy to myself as well as others.*

GAMES AND EXERCISES

WEEK THREE: THE POWER OF SELF-TRUST

1. Write about the memories, feelings, and fears around your
   first period.

2. Make a collage. Get a pile of magazines, a pair of scissors,
   a large piece of poster board and some glue. Hold the idea of
   your teenage self in your mind, while you cut out photographs, ads, words, and phrases from the magazines. Don't
   linger over the images, just cut out whatever speaks to you at
   the moment. Let the choices you make be intuitive rather than
   intellectual decisions. Spend no more than a half an hour
   cutting out the images. Now, glue them onto the backing to
   create a collage. You may linger over the arrangement and
   gluing part of the collage process for as long as you like, but
   remember to rush through the cutting out portion of the
   exercise to ensure that your choices are not conscious ones.
   Bring your collage to share with your circle next time
   you meet.

3. Continue to study the framed photo of yourself as a teenager.
   Look at it at least twice a day. Ask yourself: Who is that girl?
   Is she familiar? What are you beginning to remember about
   her? About her friends? Her environment? Her dreams?
   Her fears? (**NOTE:** Some people ignore this game. Please don't.
   It is a vital and integral part of your journey.)

GAMES AND EXERCISES

4. In the last chapter you chose your Power Woman role model
    —a woman who achieved success, created art, or made a
    difference in the second half of life. Now begin researching her
    life. Read about her and make notes. If this is someone you
    know and she is still living, you will want to interview her.
    Call her now and set up a time for the interview.

5. Each morning write an affirmation confirming your self-trust.
    Write it over and over at least 15 times. Then write it on a 3" x 5"
    card or any other small piece of paper and carry it with you
    all day. You may use the affirmations on page 79, or make up
    your own.

REMEMBER to journal and meditate daily. Notice how much
more you seem to be getting from the meditation and the journaling
as you become consistent.

THE POWER OF

Courage & Ability

"The purpose of life is to live it, to taste experience to the utmost, to reach out eagerly and without fear for newer and richer experiences."

– Eleanor Roosevelt

When I first began meditating on the Eleven Points of Power, I was constantly taken back into pre-history and the time of myth and magic. My father was a history buff. In the evenings, when all the other fathers in our neighborhood were watching television, mine poured over history books. He taught me that by studying history we could find a vision for the future. So as this course unfolded, I found my mind jumping between pre-history and the present time almost as if they were happening simultaneously.

Some scientists and mathematicians are investigating a theory that metaphysicians and science fiction writers have long believed: all time happens concurrently. This theory suggests that time is stacked like a many-layered cake. We are experiencing one layer now, but if we cut through the frosting we will see another layer of time.

Taking this into consideration, our teenage lives are happening simultaneously with our move into and through menopause. As we've been discovering, these two periods in our lives are very similar. They are both times of great hormonal change. They are both about exploration of a new self. They are also both times of new discoveries and new frontiers. They are both about coming of age. To embody all of this in our present state of awareness, we need to let the magic of circular time seep into our consciousness, or rather just below our consciousness, so that we can begin to sense the incredible potential of both our personal and societal past as it begins to infiltrate and empower us here and now.

We all have the ability to experience other levels of awareness, but we may not be conscious of it. We live in a society that teaches the opposite. We are taught to believe only what we see. What we must learn is to look past what we can see with our eyes. We need to look past the normal three-dimensional world into the mists dividing the layers of time and space. We must peer beyond the place that is familiar and safe to the place where we can uncover our ability to become all we were meant to become.

When I was forty-five, at the very beginning of my menopausal journey, I took another journey to England to be married. Because of British law and my fiancé's work schedule, I went early to establish residency. I was aware when I left the United States that this was a journey not only of the heart, but also of the soul. And it was perhaps this understanding of the spiritual initiation that I was about to undertake which enabled me to see beyond the boundaries of the ordinary world, because from the moment that I stepped foot on English soil my consciousness shifted. We were getting married in the town of Dorchester in Dorset, which is in the south. I was unfamiliar with this part of the country, and I knew little to nothing about its ancient history, but even on the first day, walking through town and along the river, I felt some kind of primordial power emanating from the ground. On the third day of my stay, I took the advice of a clerk at the inn where I was staying and went to visit the Maumbury Rings. It was there that I came in contact for the first time with the enormity of feminine wisdom and power.

The Maumbury Rings are the site of a pre-historic circle of stones. Ancient stone circles are scattered throughout the English countryside. What makes the Maumbury Rings stand out is that most of the stones, or henge monuments, are missing or buried under the ruins of a Roman amphitheatre, which was erected on the site nineteen hundred years ago. These Roman ruins are in turn now covered with centuries of earth and a blanket of green grass.

I have traveled to other stone circles in England since that first encounter, and done a great deal of research about them, but on that morning in 1990, Stonehenge was the only stone circle I had ever heard of, and I knew very little about it. Heading out to explore the Maumbury Rings, I had no idea what to expect. I was only going there, rather than investigating the home of the English novelist Thomas Hardy—which was also in the guidebook—because the woman at the hotel had been so insistent.

The walk through town and past an excavation of other Roman ruins was lovely. The sun was shining and the sky was cloudless. I was tempted to stop and explore these ruins, but I resisted the impulse and continued toward the Rings. After a few minutes, I became aware of a strange, disquieting feeling. In Italy, I'd always found the stumbled-upon ruins friendly, almost whimsical, but here they seemed out of place. I thought at first that it was just the lack of the Mediterranean sun enhancing the ancient stones, but it was more. The earth seemed as if it were rebelling against the stern bridle of Roman orderliness, as though the land was straining against the harness of an overlord. England, which I'd always thought of as proper and tame, was sending me very different signals. I had begun noticing an almost pagan sensibility in the rural people here. Now, as I pressed on toward the Maumbury Rings, I was beginning to see a parallel between the ancient ways of the people I'd met in the town and the spirit of the ground itself.

Soon I left the Roman ruins behind and passed the train station and the constabulary, which brought me abruptly back to the twentieth century. But not for long. Another half a city block and there it was looming before me. I hadn't known what to expect, of course, but I knew immediately that this huge mound of earth – at least thirty feet high and three hundred feet long and completely overgrown with the ever-present wild English grass – had to be the Rings.

It was the quintessential front lawn. I could feel the eight-year-old girl in me emerge, giggling with anticipation. I wanted to run right in and roll down the grassy slopes, but a rusted turnstile gate stopped me. The latch was unfamiliar, and I had to fiddle with it for several seconds. When I finally released it and moved through the gate, my girlish enthusiasm was muted by an overwhelming sense of awe.

Though I was no more than three feet closer to the entrance of the Rings I felt as though I were in another world and time. I stopped to read the plaque that gave me no more information than I already knew, but the simple act of reading the plaque lessened my feeling of awe and re-established my status as a tourist. I began my ascent to the entrance with a confident stride.

But as I got closer, my steps became more halting, and when I arrived at the threshold, I felt as though an invisible wall stopped me. I looked into the Rings and saw a large grass bowl the size of an American football field: nothing very spectacular, really. The sloping sides of the bowl where the bleachers were, during the Roman era, were now eroded and overgrown with a thick green carpet rising thirty or forty feet and obliterating everything from view except the crystal-blue canopy of sky.

I crossed the threshold and suddenly all sounds from the outside world ceased, replaced by a kind of hollow, swirling silence that grew increasingly intense the farther into the Rings I went. Each step seemed to swathe me in one after another layer of magic. And when I arrived at the center, I felt like I was entering the vortex of something ancient and extremely powerful.

I turned around slowly, eventually returning to my starting position. It was as if the silence rose up out of the earth to a crescendo that seemed to pull me toward the ground until I was seated cross-legged in the organic navel of the place.

The dew-wet grass soaked through my jeans, and I was thinking that maybe I should meditate, when a dark, ultra-violet mist rose from the ground beneath me and enveloped the entire space. Transparent figures bled through the mist, projected against the Rings' walls, flickering like images in an early silent film.

Women covered in red paint, some wearing deer heads with antlers, danced around open fire pits holding elaborately carved wooden wands. They raised the wands above their heads, then, with precise, powerful movements, lowered them to the ground. Drummers sat in niches carved into the sides of the Rings high above the dancers. Everyone and everything was drenched in red paint or blood. The sound of the drumming grew louder and louder. Everyone, it seemed, was female, the dancers, the drummers, the great priestesses. The blood dripped off them and clung to them. And in their faces I saw ferocity unequaled by anything I'd ever seen before.

I knew I was being allowed to view a grave and sacred rite of a civilization whose memory had been buried for thousands of years when the Romans arrived on this soil—a civilization so old that the most ancient Druids had heard only vague whispers of its existence.

Perhaps minutes had passed, or hours, or seconds, when the women, the priestesses, the drummers and dancers, the blood and the dark violet mist faded back into the deep recesses of the ancient Rings, leaving me in the Maumbury Rings of twentieth-century Dorchester. I looked at my watch. It was ten thirty-five—only five minutes since I'd entered, but five minutes in another millennium. Which one? How long ago had these fierce and potent women ruled the world? It was a time when the priests and shamans were all women; when the only thing that could maintain the human race in an untamed wilderness was the savage ferocity of the feminine energy fighting for the survival of the brood she nurtured. A time when blood linked humans to the gods, and the Great Goddess was mother of birth, life, and death, bleeding periodically, queen of the fields and the caves, guide from the life on Earth to the life after death. Wolf woman, fiercely competing with the Titans (floods, ice ages, ferocious beasts, droughts, heat, starvation, death in childbirth, infant death, disease) for the continuance of her issue. Anything and everything was sacrificed to make life on Earth succeed.

I slowly returned to my body, stood, and stretched my legs. Nothing stirred across the open green field. Not a bird or field mouse, just the still grass under the canopy of blue sky. But now I was intensely aware that the insistent pounding of aeonian drummers resided beneath the layers of history and that their ancient rhythms will beat for as long as the Earth orbits the sun. This is the pulse of feminine energy, articulated by the earliest peoples of our race and held in this cup of earth.

As I walked to the threshold to leave, I crossed paths with a young mother and her two-year-old son. He ran ahead of her through the portal where the ancient henge had stood. He squealed with delight as he toddled down the gently sloping hill into the Rings and threw himself face first onto the damp grass. I stood with his mother watching him rush into this great earthen womb. "This is a wonderful place for children," I said. "Oh, yes. Lovely," she said.

Could she feel the power here? Had she seen the dancers and the drummers and the festival of blood? Perhaps when she was a child. Maybe that was why she brought her child here now, while he was still open to the magic she may remember only in her dreams.

Though I had begun to study ancient goddess cultures before I arrived in Dorchester, this vision was the first time I realized just how powerful women have been and must be again. After this experience, I began to get a new sense of the word power. Feminine power. Feminine ability. Feminine courage. Fundamental. As creative as the act of giving birth. As comprehensive as sustaining life. And feminine courage is the cradle that holds it all.

THE RED TENT

"Women use their intelligence to find reasons to support their intuition."

– G. K. Chesterton

Women's intuitive nature is enhanced during menses. At menopause, this enhanced state of intuition moves from a cyclical occurrence to a constant state. In ancient times, childbearing women moved into sacred places during their cycles, which occurred in direct relationship to the full moon. (Even today, women who work or live in a close community find that their cycles become synchronized.)

The actual spaces where women convened differed from culture to culture. In Native American tribes, the women gathered in huts. The women of the nomadic tribes of the Middle East assembled in tents. The women in northern Europe, as in the vision I experienced, celebrated the moon and their bleeding in ceremonial earthen circles or mounds. Postmenopausal women led the ceremonies, supported by the young bleeding women. No men were allowed. Male energy was believed to lessen the power of the moon.

Virginia, a Native American friend, who lived in a Los Angeles apartment surrounded by concrete, spent every full moon chanting and praying in my garden. She would arrive at moonrise and stay until dawn. She told me that she once asked her husband to join her. I said that sounded like a good thing. She threw her head back so that her long, black hair shook and shimmered along her back.

"I was a fool," she laughed. "My mother told me this from the time of my first period, but I didn't understand until I brought Lance into the garden that night. Men sap the energy of the moon. They are not allowed."

They are not allowed. *She stated this like it was ancient law. Virginia had such a powerful presence that it was hard to doubt her.*

The cycles of the moon coincide with the cycles of the female body. When women are menstruating, we experience intense surges of intuitive energy. And when women pass through menopause, the same thing occurs. As young women, these intense surges will make us irritable as our cycles announce themselves. We often lash out, or become grumpy or depressed. As older women passing through menopause, these same surges cause angst, anger, and depression. What we are really feeling is the need to be alone with women and the moon so that we can channel our emotions into the constructive intuitive work that we are meant to be doing.

In tribal societies the men understood about the red tent. They knew that the monthly gathering of the women in the red tent was important for the entire tribe, because the women, their intuitive powers multiplied significantly by the full moon, used this time to meditate on the problems and challenges facing the tribe. Women emerged from the tent with solutions. Imagine a world in which women gather monthly to meditate to find answers for the problems of their communities and the world.

In our menopausal years, we need both solitude and the company of women to enhance our power. Nowadays men don't just naturally offer us the space and time we need, because they have no comprehension of it. So we must demand it. We can explain it to our loving male partners and hope for understanding. But if they don't understand, we must stand firm anyway and get what we need.

Questions to Ponder

- *Have you ever been called "bitchy" or described in some other derogatory way during or just preceding your period?*
- *Do you recall a time when you really wished that your partner or your children would just disappear and leave you alone during your period or your menopause?*
- *Have you felt guilty in the past for being "unable to control your emotions" during your period or menopause?*
- *In a perfect world how would you spend the days of your period or the time of your menopause?*

A Real Red Tent

At the 2004 Omega Women and Power Conference, there was a real Red Tent built in one of the smaller ballrooms at the hotel. ABC Carpet & Home, a woman-owned, earth-friendly furniture and carpet company, donated the materials and the labor to create it. It was about 1400 square feet and was made of different shades and patterns of red silk. The floor was covered with exquisite Persian rugs, and piles of beautiful pillows, mostly in tones of red. There was no schedule for the Red Tent. Conference attendees were able to spend time there whenever the desire arose. When I entered through the layers of red silk I wandered around a bit until I felt I'd found my place to rest. I laid down in a nest of the exquisite silk pillows. All around me the red silks and brocades created a luscious womb. As I lounged there, other women came and went. Some lay down, others sat. Some talked, others just stared into the candles on the small altars nestled along the billowing walls. I felt a primordial sense of belonging, and the joy and comfort of being a woman with other women in the safest place in the world for us. Our own world. Our own womb. Our own place of honor and regeneration.

On the final day, deep sadness overtook me and a small group of women watching the workers disassemble it. My wish is for all the women in the world to experience sitting in a Red Tent. Perhaps we could begin constructing them in our communities.

ANGER: A NATURAL STATE OF THE OPPRESSED

"Courage is the price that life exacts for granting peace."

– Amelia Earhart

When women realize how much of our power we've had to suppress during our lifetimes, we often find ourselves incredibly angry, and for good cause. We come into this world with huge amounts of potential. We have brains, strength, beauty, and a whole lot of creative ideas. On top of all that, we have our feminine intuitive and nurturing talents. We are magnificent beings. But early on, our social training begins. We aren't allowed to participate in some things. We're expected to "act like little ladies." And when we hit puberty, a whole new set of rules gets laid down. It's as though we're handed a restraining order. A lot of these new rules have to do with sex. As these new regulations begin to impinge on our developing personalities, anger starts to build. As the anger increases, we're told things like *anger will get you nowhere. Anger is unhealthy. Anger must be stopped. Anger isn't very pretty.* The truth is, our families and our communities are terrified of our anger. So they teach us to bury it. And when we bury enough anger for a long enough period of time, we can become clinically depressed.

In our society, we treat depression with drugs, which act to suppress our feelings. What they don't do is address the suffocated anger that is the cause of the depression. When anger is never recognized as valid, or even existent, it continues to be repressed and ignored.

We must express our anger. It takes courage to express anger in a society that is so afraid of it. We have the courage, we just have to dig down with the tools in this course and find it. The journaling, the meditation, and the games that are part of this course will help you get to this anger. But you must be willing to let it come up. Then using the light, and with the love and understanding of your circle of women friends, you can begin to heal.

ANGER DISGUISED AS RESISTANCE

Whenever you feel any resistance to doing the tools and the games of the course, take it as a sign that there is something hiding beneath the surface. It could be anger. If, for instance, looking at the photo of your teenage self bothers you, or if you don't want to "waste" the time it takes to go searching for a photo, take these as clues that you're angry about something. The anger may seem insignificant. You may think that you're just a little irritated with this course and some of the silly games that you don't really want to play. You may not want to make a dumb frame for the picture.

These are clues from your inner-self or your Spirit. She's tapping you on the shoulder and saying, "Look at that picture. Look at that girl and listen to her. She was very unhappy. She was furious. She wanted so much more than she was allowed. She wasn't respected. She wasn't loved enough."

The more you look at the picture the deeper you will go into the real feelings of that darling, wonderful girl. That is where the gold lies. Once you listen to her, once she has a chance to be heard, you will feel a release of pressure and tension that you weren't even aware you were carrying. And with that release will come a new sense of freedom.

Questions to Ponder

- *What are some of the little things that make you irritable?*
- *Do you remember being angry when you were a teen?*
- *What did you get angry about as an adolescent?*
- *What do you get really angry about now?*

YOU CAN DO IT

There are many things we know we can do. As menopausal women we have all lived forty years and more. We are all intelligent women. Most of us have supported ourselves financially at one time or another. A great many of us have raised children, made homes, and learned innumerable skills. We have done the amazing and the mundane. And in our minds we all know that we can do anything if we have to.

Yet there are some things we each dearly desire to do that we feel are impossible. It's as if there's a wall that keeps us from breaking through to our dreams. In the corporate world this wall is called "the glass ceiling," above which a woman can't rise. We all suffer from the glass-ceiling effect, whether or not we're in the corporate world.

For most of our lives, our generation of women have asked and even demanded that the glass ceiling be removed. The men who built it have not taken it away, though women have raised it. Nevertheless, the glass ceiling can't be raised or removed if we don't get rid of it first in our consciousness, where it has been firmly ensconced.

How many times has someone said to you, "Go ahead, you can do it"? How many times did you think, "That's not true"? How many times did you think, "I could do it, if…if I had more money…if I had more time…if I'd had more support from my parents when I was a child…if I'd only finished college…if I were smarter, prettier, richer, more daring"? You can add your own qualifications to the list.

It is a sad fact that as young women we were rarely told, *Go ahead, you can do it.* Even when we hear the phrase now, or as we think about having heard it in the past, there is a little voice that whispers, *No, you can't.* And then, for whatever reason our clever minds devise, we are suddenly less sure. We immediately become stupid. And from this place, it is an easy downward spiral into the comfort of our complacency.

I recently watched the 1948 classic film, *One Touch of Venus.* In it, Ava Gardner plays a statue of Venus, which comes to life after being kissed by a mortal man. At the film's climax, Jupiter drags Venus away from Earth while her mortal lover drives at breakneck speeds to rescue her. The film cuts back and forth between Venus, who is powerless against the male gods, and her lover, who risks life and limb to save her. As she waits breathlessly, he arrives in the nick of time and saves her from the jaws of destruction.

How many films have you seen with endings like this one? How many times have you sat in dark theatres or in your living room and watched the images of women waiting breathlessly while men work furiously to save them? How many of these images do we have embedded in our psyches? How do we break the pattern? How do we reconstruct our subconscious images from rescued to rescuer, and self-rescuer?

As a very young teenager I was the rescuer of my fantasies. As an older woman I know that any self-respecting woman must become her own rescuer. But though I have known that in my mind, until very recently there was still a part of me that felt I needed to be, and deserved to be, rescued. I also felt that if a man didn't rescue me, I wouldn't be as good as other women who had been. This didn't come from my conscious mind. I'm certainly not the kind of woman that anyone would suspect was waiting to be saved by a male hero. And yet, I was. I am not only my mind and my personal will, I am also a social construct made up of messages delivered in a million ways, including those on flickering movie screens. These are the mists through which we must peer to find our greater reality.

THE COURAGE TO LOOK AT OUR MIRRORS AND LIFE THEMES

As we become more and more consciously aware of our process and our ability to release the blocks to the flow of positive life energy through our bodies and our lives, we will begin to see that everything around us is a mirror of our inner life. The angry store clerk, the impatient driver, the whining friend have all been obligingly provided by our Spirit for our very own growth and development. They are like clues for our inner detective to direct us to what we need to heal or how we need to grow. The intensity of our reaction to these mirrors is in direct proportion to our need to release them. Our ability to step into the role of the detective to solve our mysteries is hindered only by our fear of what we may find. A good private investigator searches for the truth. The truth can never hurt. The truth will set us free. But to look at our truth takes courage. Often our truth-mirrors are not about healing and growth, but about acceptance and self-worth.

As we look into the mirrors that reflect our true selves, we mustn't exclude the ones that show us how beautiful and strong we are or how far we've come. Mirrors reflect our true grit, our wit, our intelligence, and our potential. Learning to respond to our beauty-mirrors takes as much or sometimes more courage than the ones showing us where we can improve.

It means we have to recognize and embrace the true wonder of our own power. Because many of us lack self-esteem, we react to beautiful mirrors with jealousy instead of joy.

Suppose you were having a difficult time with your finances and suddenly found yourself in the presence of wealthy people. If you are aware that everyone around you is a mirror of our true self, then you will see in these wealthy people a mirror of your own prosperous potential. Choose to see your own prosperity in the mirror and positive change will take place quickly.

If you choose to become immersed in self-pity because you don't have what they have, you will only become increasingly angry, jealous, and impoverished.

Courage is the key—courage to face our fears, accept our foibles, get down with our anger, recognize our magnificence, and explore the themes of our lives. Each of us has come into this lifetime with a very particular set of challenges. There often seems to be a main theme to these sets of challenges, such as money, relationships, death, love, or children. Sometimes it's a combination. These challenges are given to us to embrace in order to learn to live joy-filled lives in spite of them.

When we're young, we believe that as soon as we're grown up everything will be fine. We reach our thirties and are shocked to discover otherwise. We rail against ourselves for failing. As teenagers we create a set of expectations for our lives, only to be devastated when we learn they won't all pan out. We look at others who have what we had expected and measure ourselves against them. We see failure in our lives, and success in theirs.

My mother's life theme centered on death. She lost her mother when she was very young. Her fiancé was killed in an auto accident, which she survived. And her first-born son died when he was three years old. My mother was challenged with learning to love life and open her heart to a spiritual truth in the face of death. Many people I've met over the years have had similar challenges with death as their life's theme. Some, including my mother, refused the call to find love and joy in the midst of this kind of tragedy. Subsequently, they became bitter and desperately unhappy people. Others accepted the call, embraced the challenge, reclaimed joy after tragedy, and even came to realize that it was through the tragedy that their greatest happiness was revealed.

Though we must learn to see the reflections of ourselves mirrored by those around us, we can't expect the way other people address their challenges to work exactly the same for us. We are all unique individuals, with very specific lessons from which to learn and grow. Each of us has different themes and challenges. We must use our spiritual detective tools (journaling and meditation) to find what it is that makes our lives whole no matter what we think we are missing.

Kim, an attractive, charming, and intelligent woman in her mid-forties, works for a major airline. She has never moved into a management position, though she has the brains and the skills, because she lacks self-confidence to an almost crippling degree.

When I observe her life with the objective eye of an outsider, I see that she is challenged with the ongoing themes of self-worth and money. Her best friend is a millionaire who has a great deal of self-confidence. Kim measures herself against her friend, and when she does this, she feels even worse about herself.

Kim assumes that her friend's feelings of self-worth come from having a lot of money. She believes that if she had that much money, she would have the same self-confidence. She waits and worries and plans for the day when she will become a millionaire and gain the same self-confidence. Kim does have some very inventive ideas for moneymaking projects, but she is so stymied by her fear, that she never takes them to completion.

Kim's life challenge is to discover her own innate worth and develop her self-confidence without money. Once she does, she will find the courage to take her moneymaking plans to fruition, and though she may not become a millionaire, she will have unearthed her self-esteem and self-love. There is no prize for embracing our life's theme other than the well-being that comes with accepting and loving our lives, and knowing we are doing exactly what we need to be doing.

I once attended a meeting where the speaker talked about manifesting abundance. A woman in the audience said that she wanted to manifest a good agent so she could get a book deal just like the one her girlfriend got. It seemed her friend had received a $90,000 publishing advance. The woman in the audience wanted the speaker to tell her how she could manifest the same deal and the same amount of money.

When the speaker and others in the audience suggested other options, she made it clear that she wasn't open to self-publishing, or to getting a deal for more or less than $90,000. By refusing to be open to other possibilities, she stood solidly in the way of manifesting her particular life's plan.

She may have a book that needs to be read by others, and which, if it were just out in the world would satisfy her immensely, but as long as she refuses to recognize that her life's challenge is not exactly the same as her friend's, she blocks the door to her own joy and her own life's purpose.

Questions to Ponder

- *What are the recurring themes in your life?*
- *How do you deal with these recurring themes?*
- *Do you wish the challenges would just go away? Has wishing worked?*
- *What could you do to begin living a happy life despite these challenges?*
- *What would it mean to embrace the worst parts of your life? Do you have the courage to try?*

GAMES AND EXERCISES

WEEK FOUR: THE POWER OF COURAGE & ABILITY

1. Make a list of any 10 things at which you are really good. They can be as simple as: I'm good at making friends, or gardening, driving, being on time, skiing, making the bed. Write your list quickly. Don't give yourself time to analyze, just write the first things that pop into your mind.

   Next, following the same guidelines as for the "good" list, make a list of 10 things at which you are merely okay.

   Finally make a list of 10 things at which you are terrible.

2. Read the lists aloud to yourself, starting with the "terrible" list, then the "okay" list, and end with the "good" list.

3. Choose one of the things at which you are good and make a pretty sign that says "I am good at_____." Post it where you can read it every day.

4. Start paying attention to your dreams. Write down in your morning journaling anything you can remember from your dreams the night before. Don't analyze, just write down what you remember. It can be just a fragment. If you don't often recall your dreams you can become more aware of them by turning on your White Star before going to sleep and then asking your Spirit to help you remember your dreams. This may not work immediately, but with practice, it will.

5. Continue studying your role model. Have you found any books about her yet? Have you looked her up on the Internet? If you've found some basic biographical material on the Internet, read that but then take your research to the next level and find books about her. If you have trouble finding information about her, ask the reference librarian at your local public library to help you. There may be essays in collections or news articles in magazines or newspapers stored on microfilm. The more you read about your role model the more insights you will gain for your own Power Woman's journey. What about her younger life led to the choices she made in her older life? What kinds of events gave her the courage to do what she did, or is doing, with her life? Take some time to focus on her and begin to see what you are learning about your own life from studying hers.

REMEMBER to journal and meditate daily. Try reading one of the *Questions to Ponder* sections of the chapter before you journal and write about them. Always try to bring some of the emotional memories or feelings that arise during your journaling into your meditation for healing and transformation.

THE POWER OF

Health & Beauty

"Age is something that doesn't matter unless you are a cheese."

– Billie Burke

As we continue to discover and connect with our Power Woman, we reach the point where we must pay attention to the basics of health and beauty. Getting older does not mean that we must succumb to ill health or fading beauty. By changing our attitude and our focus we can debunk that myth. We can create radiant health, and we can redefine beauty to include our beloved new wrinkles, bellies, and grays.

"You're over the hill." I first heard this expression when I was about eight-years-old. My father said it to a colleague who had just turned forty. Everyone laughed, but under the laughter I could sense an uneasy tension. "Over the hill." A picture flashed through my mind at that moment that I've carried with me ever since of a man hurtling down a grassy hill toward the bottom where a macabre figure of death waited.

As we move into and through menopause, our bodies show signs of aging. We begin to experience aches and pains we never had before. We need glasses for reading. We gain weight more readily. Men experience these signs as well, but women have the additional biological changes of menopause, which brings on hot flashes, irritability, headaches, and memory loss. It's no wonder, with society's conventional "wisdom" and media hype, that we assume we're headed down that grassy hill toward death. But this isn't true. We are simply passing from one stage of life to another. We are experiencing the death of our childbearing selves, and the birth of our Power Woman selves. Keeping mindful of this will help us stay healthy both mentally and physically.

As Power Women, we need good health to support our work and our play. We also need to appreciate our beauty. Health—both mental and physical—and beauty—both inner and outer—are inextricably linked. Good health promotes beauty, and beauty likewise promotes good health. But it is not western society's standards of beauty that we Power Women must concern ourselves with. We will never be twenty again. To try to remain so is a waste of energy we can put to better use.

If we look at some notable Power Woman role models such as Eleanor Roosevelt, Georgia O'Keeffe, Doris "Granny D" Haddock, or Sojourner Truth, we see a different kind of beauty: a beauty born of lives well lived. All three of these women's looks are far from pretty, but they are all strikingly beautiful because they exude strength, determination, integrity, and kindness. This is not to say that a Power Woman cannot be, like Gloria Steinem, fashionable and glamorous. As twenty-first century Power Women in good health, we may change the look of aging, but that must not be our main concern.

BIOLOGICAL TRANSITIONS—THEN AND NOW

As adolescents we were awkward, gawky, clumsy and horribly insecure, grappling with the budding personalities of our grownup woman selves. As teens, we got glimpses of the exciting new life ahead of us, but our bodies and our personalities often betrayed us, making us feel out of step, and horribly flawed.

In peri-menopause and menopause, we also feel awkward, out of sorts, and yes, even clumsy at times. We find ourselves tripping over our own feet and forgetting the simplest things. This causes painful feelings of insecurity. Like the teenagers we once were, we are glimpsing something new on the horizon, our developing Power Women, but until we arrive at the other side of menopause, we will still be feeling the affects of the change and, like our teen selves, feel a little out of step and flawed.

In adolescence, we experienced the death of our child-selves and the birth of our childbearing selves. It was a hellish demanding time, but we survived it and became wonderful grown-up women. In menopause, we are experiencing the death of our childbearing woman and the birth of our Power Woman. It can be an equally challenging period, especially when we believe that the death we are experiencing is the preparation for our actual death. But when we come to understand that we are simply sloughing off the old to make way for the birth of our new self, the excitement will help us through the next step. It may still be a bit uncomfortable, but with a bright new beginning in sight, we can stand the pain and inconvenience. During childbirth, we endure labor pains because we know that a beautiful new baby will be our reward. When we understand that our peri-menopause and menopause phases will end with the emergence of a new powerful woman, we'll be able to bear the challenges with courage and even a sense of humor.

HEALTH IS THE KEY

When we were teenagers, health issues were far from our minds. We consumed sodas, hot dogs, hamburgers, and French fries, smoked cigarettes and stayed up until dawn. Health experts are coming to understand that the physical stress caused by the immense hormonal change during adolescence needs to be supported by healthy food, exercise, and plenty of rest. Once we can get youngsters to live healthy lifestyles, we should see a dramatic drop in teen depression and suicide.

Maintaining a basic health plan must be part of every woman's lifelong regimen. During the menopausal transition, remaining healthy is all the more important in order to support our Power Woman's dreams, desires, and purpose. Failing health can put a stop to the most determined of us.

A good basic health plan includes eating nutritious foods, practicing some form of weight-bearing exercise for thirty minutes at least four times a week, and lowering our stress levels. Sometimes it's hard to keep up. Some days it seems impossible to get out and walk, or to turn away from a hot fudge sundae. If you find sticking with an exercise program too difficult to do alone you may want to join a hiking group, take a dance class, or just gather a group of friends together to walk. (Indeed, this may be a great activity to initiate with your Power Woman circle.) To maintain a healthy diet there are any number of groups that you can join: Weight Watchers, Overeaters Anonymous, or check out your local health food store, which may know of a healthy-eating support group.

My friends and I often complain that we didn't have to work this hard to stay fit and healthy when we were thirty. We whine about having to do it now. Why can't there be a drug to keep us young longer? Nevertheless, our body's look and feel better when we walk everyday or go to yoga class or work out at the gym. Yes, it's hard work, but everything worth having takes discipline and effort. A healthy, resonant life is certainly worth working for.

I recommend that you read Christiane Northup's book *The Wisdom of Menopause* to supplement this chapter.

The key to good health is in our attitude toward life. The more we enjoy getting up every morning, the easier it is to eat the right food and get out and exercise. We have to disconnect from the brainwashing media that thrives on fear-based advertising, promoting ever more potent drugs to mid-life Baby Boomers. In a television commercial, a beautiful fifty-something woman who fears heart disease takes a new pharmaceutical to assure that she'll live to dance with her grandson. Article after article promises cancer from taking hormone replacement therapy and osteoporosis from not taking it. According to the media, retirement, grandparenting, and disease are the only options for women in the second half of life. We must unhook from mainstream hysteria and discover our individual body's needs, and our own heart's desires.

Questions to Ponder

- *Were you a healthy child and teen? If not, what were your complaints?*
- *How did your parents respond to illness?*
- *Do you feel good most of the time? If not, how often do you feel ill or unwell?*
- *Do you think of yourself as a healthy person?*
- *Do you think there are things you can do to improve your health? What are they?*

BEAUTY: A PLAGUE AND A BLESSING

The idea of beauty simultaneously blesses and plagues us from a very early age. Our society reveres a certain kind of beauty. As women we are naturally beautiful. Unfortunately, natural beauty is not honored in our culture. When cute, confident little girls reach adolescence they develop into insecure big girls, trying desperately to emulate magazine models. From that moment on, we devote an inordinate amount of time and money attempting to live up to a contrived standard of beauty, promulgated by a market-driven media that has little or no interest in women and their innate beauty. We spend billions of dollars every year for products that promise to make us more beautiful. And to that end we often sacrifice our health.

Between the ages of thirteen and fifty, most women compare their looks, consciously or not, with the models and movie stars who grace the covers of magazines and parade through television ads. Few women can ever hope to look like these airbrushed media dolls, but oh, how we try— the diets! the cosmetics! the clothes! It's exhausting! We all think our lives would be so much better if we just had that dress, those jeans, that hairdo, that thin body.

When we reach our forties everything starts to change. As wrinkles begin to appear, and the body begins to sag, it takes more time and more concentrated effort to repair. Some women recognize that they will never be twenty again and are relieved that now they don't have to worry constantly about how they look. Others charge into an evermore desperate search for the elixir that will help them regain a youthful face and body— some, at any cost.

Many women feel that they are failing because they can't stop the aging process, that they can't remain forever young.

Carey, a fifty-five year old writer, tells me that she is constantly berating herself for getting wrinkles, gray hair, and sore feet. She says that her thirty-year-old daughter begs her to stop, saying that this self-castigation causes her to fear and resist aging.

Carey wants to stop hating herself for aging, especially because of the way it affects her daughter, but she doesn't know how. She says that sometimes she feels almost as if it is her fault, something she did wrong to make her grow older.

The first point of power is the Power of Self-Love. When we can learn to truly love ourselves, we will be able to accept who we are and where we are on our path through this life. Then we can drop such self-destructive beliefs.

We don't want to give up on looking our best, but our best requires new standards—standards that we create ourselves, based on our unique qualities and attributes. Measuring our beauty against a sixteen-year-old model or our daughters' youthful elasticity is detrimental to our mental health, not to mention our daughters' mental health. And our mental health is one of the most important factors in maintaining our physical health and recognizing our true beauty.

JUDGING OURSELVES AND OTHERS

Women come in all sizes, shapes, and colors. Our beauty lies in our inimitability and diversity. Our expression of beauty must not be dictated by anyone other than ourselves. As teenagers, this was impossible to understand, but as powerful women in the second half of life it's imperative that we do.

As adolescent girls, we were constantly competing with our peers. Being "in" as a teenager was extremely important. Getting into the right group or clique, or being chosen for the cheerleading squad or for roles in the school play all contributed to our teenage angst. To make things worse, we had to look a certain way: thin, acne-free, with Hollywood starlet features, preferably blonde, and—in the 1950s and '60s—white. If we didn't live up to the impossible standards of "beauty" dictated by the popular girls and boys, then we were pretty miserable. Even the precious creatures that led the "in" cliques suffered from the stringent rules of the ruthless fashion guides. Seventeen magazine called the shots where I went to school.

The adolescent world has not changed much in forty years. The '90s film and short-lived TV series, *Clueless*, took us into the center of the judgmental teen years. Though the heroine had a heart of gold, she still adhered to strict fashion codes that could not be broken. The "nerd" girl had to be made over by our "caring heroine" to succeed in the world of adolescent peer pressure.

As teens we are trained to judge our sisters. It is the beginning of the "divide and conquer" strategy of the dominator society we live in. We judge everything from clothes to boyfriends. But most of all we judge physical looks. Sadly, we carry that judgment of our sisters throughout our lives. It sprang from our insecurity born of the negation of our feminine power at the moment it began to bud.

Judgment of others is judgment of self. Each flaw we find in others simply mirrors the flaws we see in ourselves. Each time a teenage girl judges her sisters, she becomes more firmly entrenched in her own insecurities; insecurities she will carry for years.

> *Ellen, a physical therapist in her early forties, told me that she caught herself worrying about what other woman thought of her clothes.*
>
> *"I realized I felt exactly the way I did in high school when I was faced with that kind of judgmental person."*
>
> *I asked her how it felt, and she said that it seemed ridiculous to still be reacting like a teenager at forty.*
>
> *Ellen made a conscious choice that day to put a stop to it. "I didn't have to be a teenager anymore. I could grow up. It was a revelation."*

Judging others is tiring. It takes energy that can be put to positive endeavors.

It keeps us in a loop of judging and being judged. At midlife, we have experience that can translate into wisdom, if we choose. Giving up judgment is one of the steps toward embracing the wisdom of our Power Woman. Beauty is a way of being, and it must not be judged—only appreciated. Once we realize this, we will accept our own true beauty and cherish it as a sacred right.

Mantra

"Watch without judgment and there is peace."

Repeat this mantra several times each day. Be aware of how you feel after saying it.

Questions to Ponder

- *Did you consider yourself pretty as a teen?*
- *Did anyone ever tell you were unattractive when you were a teen?*
- *What were your best physical attributes as a teen? Your worst?*
- *Did you have large, medium, or small breasts as a teen? Were you ashamed of your breasts? Why?*
- *Was there one girl or group of girls who treated you badly when you were a teen? If so, what did they do or say that was hurtful?*
- *Do you think you carry any insecurity from your teen years about your beauty today?*

STRESS IN THE WORKPLACE

Are you feeling stressed at work? Have you ever thought that the rigidity of a regular nine-to-five job isn't healthy? Many women, especially mid-life women, find the restrictions of the business world, with its cubicles and rigid hours, incompatible with the natural ebb and flow of their internal rhythms. Imposing false time schedules can cause undue stress. Consider finding a job you can do from home where you have more flexibility in your hours. Also working from home keeps you away from the pressures and politics of the office environment. Although women work best in community, the community must be based on feminine principles of caring, sharing, and nurturing. Boxed in cubicles and striving under the gun of deadlines and bottom-line pressure are not conducive to women's health or our beauty.

Beth is an office manager who works in a high-profile law firm. She is miserable about her life, her job, and her looks, and is convinced that she will have to stay at this stressful job until she retires at sixty-five. She suffers from high-blood pressure, and has been taking Prozac for three years. She looks much older than her forty-seven years. She has deep lines in her face, and her body lacks tone.

When I met Beth, she was sitting next to Vera. At sixty, Vera has wrinkles, but her skin is firm. She doesn't look young, but she looks vital and alive. She has a glow that makes her extremely attractive. Vera doesn't feel old. She runs her own small company that she began when she was fifty-five. She is in excellent health. She enjoys getting up every morning and going to work in a people-friendly environment that she created herself.

If we Baby Boomers are going to live well into our eighties, nineties and possibly beyond, Beth at forty-seven has plenty of time to turn her health and her looks around. But that will mean leaving the job which is out of line with her own dreams. It will mean taking the leap of faith to look inward to find the kind of work that will support her soul, as well as her physical needs. Once she does that, she will have a chance to regain her health, and this will naturally make her more attractive.

Cycles

Leslie Botha Williams has been studying women's menstrual and moon cycles for twenty years. All life forms, she says, respond to the waning and waxing of the cycles of the moon. There is a time to be active and a time to slow down. This cycle happens approximately every twenty-eight days. For pre-menopausal women, the cycle coincides with their menstruation cycle.

"But most women believe," Williams says, "that we stop cycling when we stop menstruating, and this isn't true. Instead, menopausal women cycle directly with the moon."

The days when the moon is waxing, from the new moon until the full moon, are the active times of the cycle for menopausal women. And the time to slow down is from the end of the full moon to the new moon. Both times, according to Williams, are extremely powerful and productive—if we know how to use them to our benefit, not detriment.

Mental, emotional, and physical fatigue sets in when women continue our patterns of activity during the inactive phases of our cycles, when the moon wanes. When we give up "fighting" the natural rhythms of our cycles, and trust the power of the universe, we can use the time for recharging, envisioning, becoming wise women whose knowledge, intuition, and power are based on understanding the natural order of life. Then, when the moon cycle becomes active, we can accomplish much more, because we are now in synch with and empowered by the Earth's energy surge.

"When you understand and live with the natural cycles of the universe,"
William says, "and you learn to trust the influence this cycle has on your
health and well being, you have the potential to become the powerful woman
you always wanted to be."

When we bring this awareness into our work environment, we can
actually lower the stress levels tremendously.

(To learn more, visit www.holyhormones.com.)

Questions to Ponder

- *Are you afraid of getting and looking older?*
- *How much stress do you have in your life?*
- *Do you work in a human-friendly environment? If not, why not?*

BEAUTY ROLE MODELS

"I think I've gotten better, stronger. More sexy – if that's
possible! I know now that menopause is not a death
sentence; it's a graduation."

– Patti LaBelle

We all exude divine feminine beauty. It is expressed in many different
forms. All women express this beauty in our own ways. No matter what
kinds of features or shapes we have, if we are happy and healthy, we
express aspects of this divine feminine beauty. Women appreciate the beauty of other women, and when we have achieved enough self-love we can

acknowledge this appreciation, drop the jealousy, and recognize that this is because we see ourselves in our sisters.

We all have at least one beautiful celebrity who makes us feel good just looking at her. Jackie Kennedy, Princess Diana, Princess Grace were all beautiful, revered, and loved by millions. Why? They were all princesses of one kind or another, and they each embodied a mythic expression of feminine beauty, which mirrored the mythic in other women.

Who do you think is the most beautiful woman in the world? Take a moment and get her firmly in your mind. If you want, find a picture of her. Next, think of what parts of her beauty are reflected in you. Do you have similar eyes, or hair, nose, legs? Do you smile alike, walk alike, talk alike? Do you express yourselves alike in some way? Now, take another moment and just bask in your beauty and hers. We are all beautiful. But beauty, like everything, must be nurtured and shared.

I love Sophia Loren. Above all other beautiful women, she is the one with whom I experience that mythic reflection. When I look at her or even think about her, I feel the essence of her beauty, physically, within my own body. I love to look at many other beautiful women, Goldie Hawn, Katherine Hepburn, Susan Sarandon, but they don't make me feel the way Sophia Loren does.

The difference is in how I experience myself, and my own beauty. When I look at the other three beauties, I simply see beautiful women whom I admire. But when I look at Sophia, I see myself. It's not that we look alike, but we express a similar kind of feminine energy. In Sophia, I see my own ample bosom and sensuousness, so that I can embrace my own beauty while simultaneously admiring hers. This is not about comparing myself to a movie star, but about experiencing similar expressions of the Divine Feminine.

When we realize how beautiful we are, and take the time to enhance our beauty in simple ways such as by wearing a lovely scarf, or a pretty necklace, we step out into the world emanating our own beauty. And because all human beings are attracted to beauty, we are attractive.

A shy woman in one of my circles, Marilyn, hides behind large glasses, wears her blond hair cropped short, and dresses in large clothes that conceal her shape. When we talked about our "beauty role models" in the circle, she practically whispered that her favorite beauty was Marilyn Monroe. (They even shared the same first name.) There was instant recognition from the other women in the group. The moment she said the name, "Marilyn Monroe," it became obvious. Behind our Marilyn's huge glasses was a sultry beauty. Under her oversized blouse were supple rounded breasts. Her pouty lips smiled coyly even as she blushed with self-conscious delight.

Maya Angelou is another of my favorite beauties. At seventy-six she exudes the kind of beauty that expresses a depth of femininity that we should all aspire to. Her poem about her flirtatious, beautiful, and powerful sexuality, "Phenomenal Woman," is a wonderful affirmation to bring into your life daily. Look it up at the library, bookstore or on the Internet. Make a copy of it and put it some place where you can read it. You can find "Phenomenal Woman" in *The Complete Collected Poems of Maya Angelou*. Take the time to read some of her other work for more inspiration.

Women are all beauties. We are beautiful goddesses with a purpose. As you examine your own beauty, let it help you dive deeper into the realm of your purpose. How does embracing your own beauty illuminate your emerging power and the sparks of ideas for your new life?

Questions to Ponder

- *Are you happy with your body? If not, what would you like to change?*
- *Do you dress in your own style, or do you let fashion or other people dictate style to you?*
- *Do you know what your own style is? Would you like to keep it or change it?*
- *What can you do to incorporate beauty and fashion into your own unique style?*

THE JOY OF WRINKLES

"Nature gives you the face you have at twenty; it is up to you to merit the face you have at fifty." (And beyond.)

– Coco Chanel

Yes, we get wrinkles when we get older. What's wrong with getting wrinkles? It's our society that tells us wrinkles are a bad thing. Our culture worships youth. We Baby Boomers invented the "cult of youth," and we can change it. As Power Women we can learn to love our wrinkles. When women like us believe in our worth to society, we will change society. We are the generation that came up with the idea that no one over thirty could be trusted, because we were under thirty at the time and were changing the world. Now, we're over forty. It's time to change the world again.

As long as we don't have wrinkles, we feel that we're still part of the youth culture. When we get wrinkles, the younger generation tends to ignore our presence. It's as though we become invisible. So, naturally, we hate our wrinkles. We spend billions of dollars on creams and cosmetic surgery. But nothing really works. Even after major plastic surgery, the skin eventually sags again and the wrinkles reappear. We're just going to have to embrace our wrinkles. We're going to have to honor them, and give them a place in our hearts.

Our lines are the maps of our lives to this point. Every moment of suffering and joy are etched into our faces. No one's lines are exactly the same. Everyone's wrinkles tell their own personal story. How you present your story is up to you.

Power Women require wrinkles. You can't be a Power Woman if you're thirty. To be a Power Woman you must have lived a full, interesting life. You must have experienced both suffering and joy. Your wrinkles, eyes, and smile show the world your Power Woman beauty.

Notice when advertisers illustrate the before and after pictures of women using some wrinkle-reducing product, the before picture shows the woman frowning and looking very unhappy. But in the after picture, she is smiling. Advertising people are very savvy. They know that when we smile all the lines in our face are drawn up, our skin is firmer across our cheeks, our eyes sparkle, and our laugh lines do what they are supposed to do, they make us look adorable.

Smiling forces us to use our face muscles. Using muscles strengthens them. Smile right now! Feel your mouth widening, your cheeks stretching. Now, frown. Feel your jaw slackening, your forehead crinkling. Which feels healthier? Which feels more beautiful? The old adage, "Attitude is everything," holds true for wrinkles, beauty, and health. The happier we are, the prettier we are, and the healthier we are. Force yourself to smile many times during the day and see what happens to your face—and your life.

Questions to Ponder

• *Do you hate your wrinkles?*
• *Do you want to be invisible at fifty and over? If not, what do you plan to do about it?*
• *Do you still look at sixteen-year-old models and wish you could look like them? When do you plan to give that up?*
• *How often do you laugh? How much of the day do you spend smiling?*

MAKING TOUGH CHOICES FOR YOUR OWN HEALTH

At midlife, many women find they are in stifling relationships that do not support them and haven't for years. As the children grow up and leave home, we have more time to reflect on what we want in our lives. If we haven't fulfilled our dreams, we can feel a terrible sense of loss. If our husband or life-partner fails to appreciate this loss, and rejects our pleas for understanding and emotional support so that we can start to fulfill our dreams, we feel horribly betrayed. But as awful as this may feel, at fifty or more, it may not seem worthwhile to rock the boat. We've put up with it for this long; might as well stick it out until the end. And many women do just that. But there are great health risks attached to this choice. Take the brave step now.

At fifty, Mary Ann's kids were grown, and she went back to college. She received her degree at 55 and was ready to begin her career as a research marine biologist. She was excited. She felt more alive than ever before in her life. But her husband had just turned sixty and decided to take early retirement. She felt fine about his retirement, but he wanted her to retire with him. At first she couldn't believe that he would ask this of her. For thirty-five years she had focused all her attention on him and their children. Now she thought he would understand that this was the beginning of a bright new future for her. It didn't occur to him.

She tried to explain that she had been dreaming of this all her life. But he was set on his plan and put an end to the discussion immediately. After thirty-five years of deferring to her husband, Mary Ann thought she had no choice. She was devastated as she moved away from her friends, and shelved her unborn career. She put a bright face over the pain and anguish she swallowed as she'd done so many times before.

The hurt and anger festered over the next few years. Whenever the feelings surfaced, she'd push them down again. Mary Ann's college girlfriends stopped calling after awhile. She thought she'd adapted well to the retirement life, but when she turned sixty-five she was diagnosed with clinical depression and the beginnings of dementia. Her once bright active mind couldn't survive under the constant strain of denial and repression.

Mary Ann's story could have turned out quite differently if she had had the courage to follow her heart.

Marsha, a fifty-four-year-old banker, married the boy next door when she was eighteen. He was her first and only boyfriend. They quickly had three children. Though Marsha worked all her married life, her career was never of any importance to her husband. For thirty years, she pushed her dreams and desires to the back burner, swallowed her frustration and pain and kept the family going.

When she was forty-six, something snapped. She felt like a dead person walking around in a live body. She forced herself into therapy though she was terrified. She was mostly frightened that she'd delve into herself and find nothing. "When you are told your entire life that you have no value," she told me, "you really believe that your life is only about someone else."

I asked her how she had the courage to take the step into therapy, and she said, "I thought I was dead already, so I figured, what have I got to lose." After four years, she was finally able to leave her husband. The year she turned fifty, she divorced him, lost her job, moved to a new town, and got a new job. For the first two years every day was a struggle, but she never once regretted the decision. On a trip to Cancun with a girlfriend, she found herself truly laughing for the first time in years. She knew at that moment everything was going to be all right.

At fifty-four, just four years after the divorce, she has a great job, a wonderful circle of women friends, and a new partner in her life who supports her work, honors her as the terrific woman she is, and absolutely adores her.

And she's not stopping there. She's exploring what her next step will be, open to all possibilities. Leaving her husband was the hardest, thing Marsha ever did, but the rewards far outweigh the struggle.

It takes courage to stand up for ourselves.

Questions to Ponder

- *If you are in a relationship now, do you feel honored and supported?*
- *Have you ever pushed your dreams aside to support someone else's dreams or desires?*
- *Do you have a hard decision to make in your life? If you do, what is keeping you from making it?*
- *Do you find it difficult choosing yourself over others?*

PASSION, PURPOSE, AND LONGEVITY

Women who have found passion in the second half of life tend to live long productive lives. A Power Woman feels the passion of her purpose welling into her heart and spilling into all facets of her life. Whether your passion is for art, politics, science, ecology, spirituality, healing, teaching, it is the passion that will make whatever you do worthwhile for both your-self and the people and the world around you. Being a worthwhile part of your world, making a positive difference, gives your immune system a huge boost. A fulfilled and joyous heart promotes holistic health.

Although the life expectancy in the nineteenth and early twentieth centuries was fifty years, the most prominent women in the anti-slavery and women's suffrage movements lived much longer. Harriet Beecher Stowe and Susan B. Anthony lived to be eighty-six; Sojourner Truth and Elizabeth Cady Stanton lived to be eighty-seven; Julia Ward Howe died at ninety-one; and Harriet Tubman expired at the grand old age of ninety-three. Most of these women worked right up to their deaths, driven by the passion of their mission. They faced immense adversity, some of them starting life as slaves, others jailed for their beliefs. Whatever their hardships, their sense of purpose gave them the grit to continue.

As you focus on your health, give your imagination free reign to explore what you might do with the rest of your life. When you come upon an idea, journal about it, and then listen to your heart. Does this idea fuel your passion? If so, you're on the right track.

FUN, FUN, FUN

Never forget the simple ingredient of fun.

A Power Woman must have fun to ensure both her health and beauty. Enjoy yourself with good friends and alone. Do things you love to do. When we were in our twenties fun usually meant drinking a lot and staying up all night. It may be nostalgic to look back at those times, but it probably isn't what you would consider fun at this time in your life. And it wasn't very healthy even then.

Instead, why not get together with a group of friends for a bike ride and picnic, or a hike, horseback riding, or playing games that stimulate your mind. But make sure that your fun is good-spirited. Play games for the fun of playing, not to win at all costs. Chat with friends over a glass of wine, but don't gossip about or belittle others. Make jokes, but not at the expense of others. And above all, laugh a lot.

Health, beauty, and happiness are inextricably linked. The color in your face after a brisk walk makes you look beautiful. The color is evidence of good, healthy blood flow. Exercise keeps blood pressure down and morale up. Smiling keeps our faces youthful. Enjoying living in our bodies is an important key to living long, productive, and active lives. Having fun with friends, keeping our minds active, and loving others, and ourselves bring beauty, health, and happiness into our daily lives. And every day is a day to recognize our own beauty, joy, and good health.

GAMES AND EXERCISES

WEEK FIVE: THE POWER OF HEALTH & BEAUTY

1. If you don't already, begin doing weight-bearing exercises four times a week for at least 30 minutes. Weight-bearing exercises include walking, running, weight lifting, dance, and yoga. (Swimming is a non-weight-bearing exercise, but has other healthful benefits.)

2. Spend some time "women watching." Go to the mall, the gym, the store, wherever there are a lot of women. Sit down and watch. Gaze without judgment at the women as they pass by. Appreciate each one for her own particular beauty.

3. Throughout each day, repeat the mantra—"Watch without judgment and there is peace."

4. Have a Venus Day (Spa Day) – You can do this in different ways depending on your pocket book and your preference. Whatever way you choose, this is a day to honor your body with the spirit of the love goddess, Venus. Go to a spa for a facial, steam bath, and/or a massage. Or trade a facial and/or a massage with another member of your circle or with a girlfriend. (Do each other on separate days so that you each get the luxury of your own Venus Day.) If you are more comfortable alone, give yourself a facial and take a relaxing bath with aromatherapy oils, soft lighting, and gentle music. Or create a Venus day of your own invention.

   In your circle you may even want to pair off and massage each other's feet.

GAMES AND EXERCISES

5. After you read Maya Angelou's poem, "Phenomenal Woman," write a poem of your own about yourself. Bring it to share with your circle.

6. Look through the clothes in your closet. What clothes support your beauty? What clothes don't support your beauty? Do you have clothes from a time in your life when you were particularly unhappy? Do you have clothes that make you look dumpy, or boring, or just plain awful? When you've evaluated your clothing, give all the clothes that don't support your beautiful emerging Power Woman self-image to a charitable cause.

7. Healthy outside is healthy inside. Is there a place in your house that is a mess? A junk drawer, your desk, your dresser drawers? Choose one messy place in your house and clean it up. Get rid of what you don't need, and organize what you do need. Be brave. Be ruthless. As you tidy your external mess you are simultaneously cleaning toxins from your body and your soul.

8. Continue learning about your Power Woman role model.

REMEMBER to journal and meditate daily. Is your journaling beginning to take a new form? What are some of the new sensations you are experiencing in your meditation? If you aren't journaling and meditating you may be finding the work more difficult than it needs to be. These tools are your best friends on this path. Don't leave them behind.

THE POWER OF

True Wealth

"Life begets life. Energy creates energy.
It is by spending oneself that one becomes rich."

– Sarah Bernhardt

T rue wealth is held in the cradle of our heart's wisdom and compassion. This is the entrance to unlimited abundance for all Earth's children and ourselves. Here, the gold waits to be scooped up, enjoyed, and shared.

As we continue this journey toward embracing our Power Woman, we find ourselves in the realm of money and prosperity, preparing to accept the Power of True Wealth. Material wealth and money elicit an odd mixture of sensations in most people: excitement, disdain, fear, envy, jubilation, anger, tightening in the chest or belly, cringing, and sometimes a feeling of expansion and acceptance. Positive feelings and sensations allow us to know real prosperity, just as negativity forces us into poverty. In this chapter we will find new ways to envision money and wealth so that we can support our emerging Power Woman and her plans for the future.

The word money is one of the most formidable in the world, ranking right up there with love and God. Money carries in its five letters the rise and fall of empires, the hopes and dreams of the strong and meek, the fear of failure and starvation, and the excitement of success and new beginnings. We want and need it; we hate and rebuke it. With enough money, our lives often—but not always—run more smoothly. When we have a lot of money we receive more respect. We envy those who have the most, and we fear those who hold the purse strings. Many people worry, with good reason, that money has taken the place of God in the modern era.

In our culture, having lots of money means having power over others. As we redefine power on this journey, we must redefine and re-envision money by learning the Power of True Wealth. A Power Woman eschews all that causes pain and suffering in the world. And right now money, or its lack, causes more pain and suffering than almost anything else. But that hasn't always been true.

MONEY IN THE REALM OF THE SACRED MOTHER

In pre-history, money was sacred. It lived in the realm of the Great Goddess and was part of the sacred dance of life. Money is actually nothing more and nothing less than the energy shared between people for the purpose of surviving and thriving on the planet. That exchange began when the first tribes met and shared the bounty of their hunting and gathering and progressed as we settled down in farming communities. You give me some grain, and I'll give you a cow. Your grain will help feed my village; my cow will help feed yours. The grain and the cow both come from the womb of the Mother. The Divine Mother was the Earth and all that she produced was sacred.

As humanity progressed, we discovered precious metals but the connection to the sacred was no less holy. In my book, *Money is Love: Reconnecting to the Sacred Origins of Money*, I write:

> When metals were introduced during the Iron Age, jewelry, cauldrons, and goblets began to be made from the most precious metals—copper first, then gold and silver. The finest of these metallic art objects were created as gifts for the gods and goddesses. Because human beings had always known the interconnectedness of all things, material and spiritual, the discovery of metals only deepened that understanding. The sun and moon were not representative of gods, but the gods themselves. The lunar goddess and the sun god lived within the moon and the sun, not as separate entities, but as integrated spirits. Gold and silver metals were understood to be extensions of the Divine spirits of the celestial divinities. Because of the sacred origin of gold and silver, these metals were initially used only in tribute to the gods. Depending on the culture, the gold and silver were deposited on an altar in a temple erected to the god, or as in Celtic societies, given directly to the god or goddess by dropping the gold and silver, in whatever shape, jewelry, goblets, coins, into sacred bodies of water. Wishing wells are a remnant of that ancient practice.

As we moved into the historic period, approximately five thousand years ago, dominator city-states were formed, and the patriarchal model moved into place. To gain and maintain power it became necessary to pay people to go to war against their neighbors to steal their land and wealth. Since it wasn't practical to pay marching soldiers with stores of grain or heads of cattle, coins became the new form of payment.

At the same time, abstract thinking was taking center stage. Human thought processes were becoming less literal, and our obsession with symbols began. This caused a crack in the sacred oneness of the material and spiritual realms, and money, which was still held sacred, became the bridge between the two. This was displayed symbolically by imprinting the likeness of a god on one side of a coin and the likeness of a king or chieftain on the other.

Money changed form over time. The European merchant class in the late Middle Ages invented checks. With the American Revolution came the wide spread use of paper money, and by the end of the twentieth century, money became plastic, and now it is quickly becoming virtual. But on the $1 bill of the United States, there still exists a remnant of money's original sacred connection. On the back, you will find the seal of the United States, opposite an unfinished pyramid topped by the "Eye of Horus" or the "All Seeing Eye of God." Above the pyramid is the Latin phrase *Annuit Coeptis*, "God has favored our undertakings." Below the pyramid is written *Novus Ordo Seclorum*, or "New Order of the Ages."

MONEY IS ENERGY

Money has had no real value since we left the wheat-and-cattle standard a millennium ago. Even gold and silver have no value except that which human beings assigned to them during Neolithic times. And forty years ago, the gold standard was discarded. If money has no actual worth, why does it have so much power?

Money is the energy people exchange for the purpose of surviving and thriving. When you hold a $100 bill, or the equivalent in another currency, you can sense the energy. It is the energy to create, to do, and to bring forth. But if money is energy, why are we always afraid that there won't be enough? After all, energy is limitless. It is all in the way we think. We believe there is a limit to the amount of money existing in the world and that belief makes it so. In our society, the amount of the money held and directed by the dominator is directly proportionate to his power. Therefore, for the dominators to maintain power over others, they must keep the illusion of limited funds alive.

In quantum physics, it is understood that energy responds directly to thought. When looking for quarks, a particle of energy smaller than an atom, scientists discovered that the quark would appear in the exact place they looked for it, though it wasn't there previous to the scientist's decision to look in that spot. This illustrates how human thought directs the movement of particles of energy.

Russell Schofield, a scholar of metaphysics and a visionary, taught that "thought directs energy and energy follows thought." This is exactly what happens in the Yin-Yang Energy Meditation we do each day. As we direct the light to move through our bodies, we are directing the movement of energy. We can direct the flow of the energy we call money in exactly the same way.

The collective thought of the dominator society has conspired to create a world where there is a limited amount of money that can be fought over and won. In the pre-dominator culture, collective thought was driven by the Divine Feminine principles of nurture and abundance for all. And now, because money is energy, we can return it to its Divine purpose by changing our thoughts and opening our hearts and minds to the truth that there is unlimited abundance that can support all the children of the Earth.

In *The Kaballah of Money*, Rabbi Nilton Bonder interprets the Talmud as saying, "True wealth is abundance that does not create scarcity." As we are able to embrace the concept that money is energy and energy is limitless, we can bring "True Wealth" into our reality. And as we Power Women help to bring honor and respect back to the feminine principles, we will help transform the energy of money from a tool of division and destruction to its original intention of nurture and healing for all.

WOMEN AND MONEY

Because women have been part of the dominated class for the past five thousand years, we have had very little participation in money and how it is distributed. Rianne Eisler tells us in *The Chalice and the Blade* that in pre-historic times, the people of "Old Europe" lived in what she describes as partnership societies. Names and traditions were passed down through the female family line, but wealth or property did not pass matrilineally because ownership as we know it did not exist. All belonged to the Divine Mother. Even today, Native Americans, along with most of the surviving indigenous cultures of the world, continue to believe that the Earth belongs to no one. We belong to the Earth.

When the dominator model of society began, women—once respected and equal members of society—were relegated to lowly servitude. Older women, once revered elders, medicine women, and tribal shamans, became the most useless members of society. Only childbearing women had worth, and that worth lasted only as long as they could deliver male children into their husband's line.

Having little or no worth in society, women lived in constant fear for their survival. Until the twentieth century, few women had means for supporting themselves. Most were completely beholden to the men of their communities for their livelihoods. A woman without a husband lived with her father or brother, joined a convent, or became a prostitute.

No wonder fear surrounds most women's experiences with money. It has been the sword hanging over our heads for millennia. Now, after little more than a century of women's activism, we find ourselves in the workforce, struggling to carve a place for ourselves in the male-dominated world of finance. It's not an easy fit. Over the past thirty-five years women have been making more money, but not necessarily enjoying the process. Some have an easier time than others learning and participating in the patriarchal model of business and finance. Nevertheless, although a lot of women have learned to play the game, I have met very few who truly enjoy it. Making a killing in the market just doesn't satisfy women the way it gratifies men. We have different priorities.

Making a good living doing fulfilling work must be our goal. And we should expect and desire to continue working at what we love throughout our Power Women years.

At seventy-five, Teresa is a tall, white haired woman with awe-inspiring dignity. She still holds the job she's had for over twenty-five years in the dean's office of a major Ivy League university. Her children want her to retire and take some time to rest. Although the work is sometimes tiring, Teresa told me she is loath to give it up. She loves her interaction with students. She feels that she is able to give them advice they don't get any place else. She said she is the only one of her friends who still has a job. "They all keep busy with their volunteer work," she said, "but they seem fragmented. They don't have any real purpose in their lives like I do." She said she was very happy that she has continued being part of the vital work force.

Teresa is a natural Power Woman. At seventy-five, she does not yet consider herself a Crone. To quit work would be quite unhealthy for her.

Volunteerism is the socially acceptable way for women over fifty to "keep themselves busy." But volunteering doesn't pay. And when a person isn't paid for her work, she tends to feel unnecessary. When people feel that they aren't necessary they have no real sense of purpose. Although volunteer work has historically been considered "good work," it doesn't pay the bills. Nor does it give a person the same sense of satisfaction of work well done as when a paycheck comes at the end of the week.

We live in a worldwide marketplace. Since money is an exchange of energy between people, when a woman works and gets no energy back from the marketplace, she feels as though she is living outside the circle of life. And being on the outside, she has no real purpose in society. Money is the energy we get for work. Therefore, women's work needs to be paid for, whatever phase of life she is in.

Volunteer work has a place in our Power Women lives, which we will touch on later, but volunteer work must be done along with, not instead of, our paid for work.

Questions to Ponder

- *How have you gotten money in your life?*
- *Have you always earned your own money or did you get some, or all, from a spouse, a parent, or an inheritance?*
- *How do you feel when someone gives you money?*
- *How do you feel when you make your own money?*
- *Do you believe that housework and raising children are jobs that should be paid for?*

DADDY, MAY I HAVE MY ALLOWANCE, PLEASE?

As little girls, most of us received allowances. Some of us were expected to perform chores to earn our allowances. Some of us got summer jobs when we turned sixteen, while others spent our summer days at the pool. But for the most part girls in the '50s, '60s, and even into the '70s, weren't taught about earning a living or paying bills or even starting savings accounts. It was simply taken for granted that we would marry men who would support us.

Men handled the money in a majority of Baby Boomer households. Though my mother paid the bills, she was quite firm in letting me know that Daddy was in charge of the money. And I believed her, because he paid me my allowance. Some weeks I would have to beg and cry to get my allowance because my father would be in one of his moods. And often I wouldn't get it at all.

Sarah, a fifty-five-year-old librarian, told me how she was trained to get money as a child. "Just before my father arrived home from work, my mother would remind me to go get my money. When I heard the car driving up I would stand by the door and wait for him to come in. Then as soon as he'd take off his coat, I'd reach in his pants pocket and pull out a handful of change. When I got older he started carrying paper money in his pocket. After I'd take the money, he'd pick me up and give me a big hug and kiss."

Putting her hand in her father's pocket always made Sarah feel strange, and it wasn't until she was in her forties that she realized the sexual implications of that action. As a result, she has always had a sense that money and sex were intimately linked. She has never been married, and a man has never supported her.

Money and sex can be and often are linked. Most of us were taught that when we give sex to men we get money. The "nice" girls married the men who gave them money for sex, and the "bad" girls didn't.

When I look back at my childhood and teen years, the only female characters in films or television I can remember who actually made money were prostitutes, dance hall proprietresses, and actresses.

Annette Funicello was a role model for women old enough to remember the original "Mickey Mouse Club." Annette didn't even have a last name until she grew up and starred in beach movies. For the millions of girls who adored her, she was just Annette. Did we ever see Annette pay for anything? Did she ever have a summer job? I don't think so. She certainly never bought a soda or a hot dog. She never spoke of making a living. She was just sweet, and her father and her boyfriends paid for everything.

"I Dream of Jeannie" offered another disturbing role model prancing across our TV screens. In this '60s television show, a woman, dressed like a harem dancer and living in a glass bottle, did everything in her power to make her man's life good. Jeannie never paid for anything. She didn't own anything. In fact she didn't even belong to herself, she was owned by her "master." With these kinds of role models it's not hard to understand why so many women are at a loss when it comes to personal finances.

Those of us who came into our adolescence in the '70s were a little luckier. We could emulate Mary Richards in "The Mary Tyler Moore Show," a strong, intelligent woman, who worked for a living, had her own apartment, and paid her own way. However, at the same time Edith Bunker, in "All in the Family," bumbled through our living rooms reminding us that no matter how ridiculous men might be, they ruled the roost and controlled the pocket book.

Questions to Ponder

- *Did you get an allowance as a teen? How much? What did you spend it on?*
- *Did you do chores or work for your allowance?*
- *Who controlled the money in your childhood home?*
- *Did your parents teach you about bills, checking accounts, and handling money in general?*

LAKSHMI—THE HINDU GODDESS OF WEALTH

In Hindu mythology, Lakshmi, also known as Shri, is the goddess of all that the material world offers to humanity. The legends say that all women of the world are forms of Lakshmi, and that where Lakshmi presides there is prosperity, virtue, righteousness, truth, and compassion.

One of the Lakshmi myths begins when Devendra, King of the Gods, carelessly allows his horse to trample Lakshmi's lotus blossom necklace that is lying on the riverbank. The great sage Durvarsa is so incensed by this lack of respect for the gracious Mother of All, that he puts a curse on Devendra so that he may never see Lakshmi again.

But this curse on Devendra deprives the entire Earth of Lakshmi's presence. Without the goddess of wealth and compassion there is great suffering throughout the land. There is not enough food for all the people. Only the kings dine on fine foods served on golden plates. The demons are happy to see this division between the rich and the poor. They side with the kings and celebrate their greed.

Soon the kings realize that their greed cannot sustain them. Without Lakshmi, the Earth is parched. No food can grow, and even the mightiest rulers have nothing left. They turn their backs on the demons and appeal to the gods to intervene to bring Lakshmi back.

It is revealed that Lakshmi now resides under the sea of milk. It will take the power of all the gods, mortals, and even the demons to churn the sea of milk and return her. After much politicking, the gods convince the demons that once Lakshmi is restored to heaven, the kings will regain their wealth and will turn to them again to support their wars and greed.

All the gods, mortals, and demons agree to work together to churn the sea of milk. They work for many days, but to no avail. At last, just as they are about to give up, Lakshmi arises on a red lotus blossom with golden coins falling from her hands. All are elated by her presence. She brings ambrosia to heal the land. There is great rejoicing, but quickly the demons steal the ambrosia. The celebrating stops as the gods fight the demons to reclaim the ambrosia. The great God Vishnu, who is the preserver of the universe, comes to the rescue, disguised as a beautiful seductress. He takes the ambrosia from the demons, and then instructs the gods and the demons to sit down in two lines so that he can share the ambrosia equally with all of them. But this is a trick. He fills the cups of the gods with ambrosia, but the cups of the demons he fills with poison. With the demons finally gone there is great celebration, as Lakshmi bestows health and prosperity on the land once more.

It's interesting to note that even the demons are integral in bringing Lakshmi back to Earth. Because the demons hold power over the parched and barren land, they are necessary in the return of the Great Mother Lakshmi. Yet they must be tricked into the game by the gods, who know that their delight in war and the games of greed and seduction, are also their downfall.

In our society, the demons are playing their role in churning up the sea by showing their hand so obviously in the wars, politics, and corporate scandals that abound. As we Power Women and everyone who loves goodness and truth own our power, we are joining the forces churning the sea of milk, and in the final act, we will depose the demons.

Like Lakshmi, women hold the key to wealth and prosperity for all the Earth. We are the mothers. We are the gift givers, for life is the greatest gift. The milk that nurtures our young also nurtures the Earth.

SHRINGING

Whenever you find yourself in a time of scarcity you can call the goddess Lakshmi or Shri into your life. To do this, simply chant the word "Shring" 108 times.

You may chant in any pitch or tone. Toning is extremely powerful. It opens a resonance in both your body and spirit and allows you to enter into a deeper harmony with the world and the universe. You can use a Mala, which is a rosary-like string of 108 counting beads plus one anchor bead. Malas are often made from wood or seeds, but can be assembled from any kind of bead, and strung on a heavy cotton thread. They can be purchased in stores that sell sacred objects or imports from India, Nepal, Tibet, or Thailand. Both Buddhists and Hindus use Malas in their prayer practices.

Questions to Ponder

- *Who are the demons that keep you from enjoying the prosperity of Lakshmi?*
- *How can you convince your demons to join in the resurrection of your own prosperity?*
- *Can you envision yourself rising, like Lakshmi, to restore balance and goodness in your own life? Try.*

THE YOGA OF MONEY

Knowing that money is connected to the sacred and that money is energy may be theoretically interesting, but bringing it into practical use is another matter. For women in twenty-first century Western culture, divinity and quantum mechanics are a little hard to focus on when we're also trying to buy groceries and pay the bills. But as Power Women we can allow prosperity into our lives once we understand the process. The key is to step back from fear and focus our attention on our money with the intention that it will flow easily and effortlessly through our lives.

The key here is paying attention to our money. Too often we spend our money in a completely unconscious state. Notice the next time you're at the checkout line at the grocery store. Do you pay attention to the actual monetary transaction? Probably not.

We tend to go unconscious when spending money, because thinking about money brings up everyone's primal survival fear. This fear is so deeply seated in most of us, it makes us want to ignore money altogether. The psychology seems to be that if we pretend money doesn't exist, it can't hurt us, and somehow we'll have enough. For a great many of us in western society, this does work, but only marginally. With more attention on money and less fear of it, we can also have enough to support our dreams and our life's work, and live at peace as well.

I teach a workshop called "The Yoga of Money" in which I use the metaphor of practicing yoga to explain how we can find peace and prosperity by putting our attention on our money, the way yoga practitioners concentrate attention on their breath.

Yoga is a spiritual discipline that seeks inner peace through the practice of strengthening our physical, mental, and emotional bodies. In yoga, we don't force our bodies into the yogic postures, we focus on our breathing, so that little by little, gently, our bodies become stronger and more limber. Eventually, our bodies move into the breath's rhythm and our postures become effortless, creating a feeling of inner peace.

When we put our attention on our money the way we put our attention on our breath in yoga, little by little, gently our bank accounts will become stronger effortlessly, also creating a feeling of inner peace.

Questions to Ponder

- *Who handles the money in your household?*
- *Do you enjoy paying bills? If not, why not?*
- *Do you wish someone else would deal with the bills?*
- *What does money mean to you?*

TURNING MONEY INTO LOVE

By the time we reach midlife, a lot of us have experienced the power that negative and positive thoughts have in our lives. We are held hostage by negative emotions and set free by positive ones. But we rarely make the connection that our thoughts and feelings directly affect the amount of money we have.

This is because most of us still have denial about money. We wonder, when we do think about it, if we have the ability to get money for ourselves or if we deserve to be prosperous. Our spirits are so clogged with negative emotions, such as shame, guilt, doubt, self-hate, lack of self-worth and self-esteem, along with anger, greed, and revenge, that the naural flow of prosperity has a difficult time seeping in, let alone flowing in.

Each of us has some amount of all these emotions. We all cling to deep-rooted belief systems that come from our families and our society. Our families each have unique money challenges, and also most of our parents or grandparents lived through the Great Depression, and the scars from that era emotionally crippled an entire generation. This generation handed that hurt down to us. In order to open the floodgates and let in the abundance, we must recognize both personal and societal issues and release them. We can do this by using our tools of journaling and meditation as well as the special games and exercises for this chapter. We can peel away another level of negative belief and reveal some new layers of our own truth based in the emotions of love, self-esteem, caring, sharing, gratitude, and our well-deserved prosperity. Focus your morning journaling on money and see what you learn about your parents' and society's influence on your money consciousness.

Along with your journaling, try introducing the mantra "Money is Love" into your daily life. Simply by repeating this simple affirmation again and again, you bring your attention to money with the intention of stripping away the negative thoughts and emotions about money, releasing your fears and transforming it into love.

MONEY IS THE BLOOD OF THE PLANET

Money circulates the planet constantly. It changes form from dollars into rubles into pounds, euros, yen, etc., as it crosses borders, yet it continues to move. This is the nature of money. Money—like rivers and streams—

travels throughout the planet and affects everything it touches in some way. Blood carries nutrients through the body to keep it healthy. When the blood is diseased, the body becomes diseased. Money flows through the world as blood surges through the body. Money carries with it the ability to provide for all the world's needs, but when it is contaminated, the entire world becomes unhealthy. To heal a person with a blood disease, the blood must be cleansed or a transfusion administered.

If one by one, we Power Women begin to change the money that moves through our hands and our bank accounts into love, joy, abundance, and goodwill, the money itself will become healed. Like a blood transfusion, we will begin to infuse the Earth's money supply with love. Then the love-infused money will begin to infect the entire money supply of the world. When Money *as* Love circulates, it affects the population and the healing process begins. Love becomes the connecting tissue that reunites money with the sacred. Gradually, we can invite our families and communities to join in the effort.

PUTTING MONEY AS LOVE TO WORK FOR YOU

Our wise, emerging Power Women selves know the folly in the *bottom-line* mentality of our current culture. The truth that money is part of the Divine lives deep in the cellular memory of our sex. We know that the real *bottom-line* is love and caring. Because we have depended for our money on men for thousands of years, our talent for effortlessly allowing abundance into our lives has lain dormant. It's time to change that. It's time to connect with money directly. We have to cut out the middle*man* by starting our own businesses, banks, and institutions, trusting and following our instincts instead of the male financial model.

As you move closer to understanding your life's purpose, you may find yourself saying, "yes, but how can I make money from this?" Or, "how can I find the money to support this new way of life?" When you put your attention on your money and turn your money into love with your thoughts, you will find that doors open and ways appear that you've never imagined. Transforming money into love will enhance not only your financial life, but also everything else in your life. Paying bills will become a joy as you send love-money to the gas and electric companies, the phone company, your credit cards, and, yes, even to the IRS.

Money is the staple of life. Money was originally food, and now it buys the food, shelter, and clothing that support life. As we women who bear and raise children and take care of families know, you don't deny food, shelter, or medical help to any part of your family. When a woman deprives her children of any of these things it is considered aberrant and even criminal behavior, even when she can't provide for them. But when the entire human race denies food, shelter, and medical care to huge portions of the human family, it is considered normal.

This dysfunctional concept must change. We must *be* that change.

Questions to Ponder

- *Would you like to change the way money flows through your life?*
- *How do you intend to support yourself in the second half of your life?*
- *Do you think you have to retire at sixty-five even if you like your job?*
- *Do you have a nest egg? If not, what can you do to begin to accumulate one?*
- *Do you invest in stocks and bonds? Do you consider how and for what purpose your money will be used before you invest in a company?*

GAMES AND EXERCISES

WEEK SIX: THE POWER OF TRUE WEALTH

1. Start your journaling each day while working with this chapter using the line: "When I think about money I often feel…" and go from there. Don't worry if your writing veers away from money. Just start with the idea of money.

2. Call Lakshmi into your life by Shring-ing at least once a day. If you are currently in need of a financial boost, consider Shring-ing two to three times a day. This often gives you the kick-start you need to open up to the flow of Divine abundance. Refer to page 135 for directions.

3. Take all the money out of your wallet. Turn on your white and deep violet light energies and pour the light through your arms, into your hands, and out into the money. This will cleanse and transform the negative energy that surrounds the money into the energy of love, joy, goodwill, and abundance for all.

4. Make a list of ten ways you think it would be FUN to make a living.

5. Write "Money is Love" on your checks, credit card slips, and deposit slips. In the three or four seconds that it takes to write "Money is Love," you create a crack in the wall of fear separating you from your own Divine prosperity. For those few seconds, fear drops away, love takes its place, and you are elevated into a higher state of being.

Next: As you hand your check or credit card slip to the clerk, become aware that you are momentarily in a state of grace. Now, experience sending money as love through this cashier, into the cash register, and out into the world.

6. Look at your teenage picture every day. Ask her how she would like to make money.

REMEMBER to journal and meditate daily. Try to focus your journaling on money and what money has meant to you in your life. Use your meditation to begin to heal the places in your physical body where you hold feelings of lack, undeserving, greed, fear of loss, and helplessness. Send light energy into all of your monetary transactions.

T H E   P O W E R   O F

Our Own Direction

"...the reason we haven't found our grail, the key to who we are as women, is because we look for it in a world of false power, the very worlds that took it away from us in the first place. Neither men nor work can restore our lost scepter. Nothing in this world can take us home. Only the radar in our hearts can do that."

– Marianne Williamson

U p to this point we have been laying the foundation for our Power Woman, creating a loving, trusting, creative, able, courageous, and healthy woman, who can support herself and her dreams. Now it's time to delve into our souls to discover those dreams and peel away the blinders that have kept us from recognizing them. We must use "the radar in our hearts" to find our direction.

Direction is a dynamic word. In its most innocuous form it is simply the way that something or someone faces or moves, the common directions of up, down, left, right, diagonal, outward, inward, across, and around. But when we internalize the idea of direction, it takes on more weight. We can delve down, aspire up, move left or right in our politics. We can spiral down emotionally. We can lift up our hearts.

When I was in France, I was always amused by the traffic signs that read "Toutes Directions," All Directions. I tried to imagine going in "toutes directions" simultaneously. I was so intrigued by the idea that I took a photograph of one of these signs and framed it when I returned home. It still hangs in my office, reminding me to focus whenever I am fragmented and my mind is going in "all directions."

When I lived in Italy, I never asked for directions. Italians, I learned, hate to let anyone down, so even if they don't know the directions you've asked for, they make up something to be polite. The combination of my minimal knowledge of the language and their etiquette enabled me to see parts of Rome I'd never planned on exploring.

Whose directions have guided your life? As children, it was natural that our parents directed us. When we reached adolescence, we began to balk at their direction. We believed that as adults, we would become the directors of our own lives, and we couldn't wait to get there. But instead, when we became adults, we acquired other directors—our mates, our children, our government, our bosses, and society in general. Now, at midlife, as when we were teenagers, we are balking again. We want to direct our own lives.

WHO IS DIRECTING THE DIRECTION WE'RE GOING?

Throughout our lives, most of us have had a pretty clear idea of the direction we were headed. Getting a job and a mate, raising children, sending them to college to get a job, a mate, and children. Though we may resist the idea that something has directed our lives other than our independent thoughts and desires, the truth is that we are members of a society which outlines highly specific roles for women to play.

The direction I believe most of us want to move in, as we step over the threshold into the second half of life, is one of respect, power, and independence within a loving, sharing, and caring community.

So, how do we do it?

We create a new direction for ourselves as women in the second half of life. We find like-minded women and create our own caring communities in which we can nurture our budding power. And we become the directors of our own lives.

Questions to Ponder

- *What direction did you want your life to take after getting out of school?*
- *Did your life go in the direction you hoped for? If it didn't, why not?*
- *What direction did you dream of heading but didn't dare believe it was possible?*
- *Who were some of the directors in your life? Parents, children, spouses?*
- *Did you follow others' directions even when they went against your own dreams?*
- *What would you have done differently in your life if you had been more assertive?*

OUR DIRECTION, NOT SOMEONE ELSE'S DIRECTION

To grab the reins and position our lives in an exciting, fulfilling, and powerful new direction we need to unlearn some of our early programming. As teenagers, most of us had no direction other than that foisted upon us by parental and social expectations. Even those of us who had some idea of who we wanted to be were reminded daily that husband and family came first. I wanted to be an actress. I went to college and majored in theatre. I truly believed I was directing my own life. But when I thought I was pregnant during my sophomore year, I allowed my parents to direct me into marriage. As bold as I was, I didn't have enough will to fight my parents and society, so I married the guy and pretended to myself that I hadn't succumbed.

Every one of us has an inner-voice that whispers to us, saying things like "don't go to the college your parents want you to go to." "Go live in India for a while." "You know you love history; don't major in science." "Don't get married, go to New York to be a dancer." When we're teens, our inner voices speak to us in day- or sleeping dreams. Everyone hears the inner voice, but few of us realize that we have the right, the obligation, to listen to it.

Victoria, fifty-six, wanted to be a teacher, marry a loving man, and have four children. In college she met Tom and married him just after graduation. But fourteen days after the wedding he was drafted and sent to Viet Nam for two years. Those were the two best years of Victoria's life. She started a teaching career and settled into her own apartment.

Then, Tom returned from the war. While Victoria had been discovering her own direction and finding satisfaction in her career, her husband had spent two years in combat, anticipating a homecoming to a woman who would wait on him, bow to his wishes, and follow his commands. He demanded that Victoria

*stop teaching, despite her years of training, and insisted that
instead of four, as they'd agreed, they would have only two
children. Victoria was shocked.*

*When she threatened to leave, he blackmailed her with his
war experiences. "He told me over and over how he had gone to
war and that he'd done it for me and his country. He was really
suffering a lot when he first came home, too, with nightmares
and stuff, and I felt so bad for him.*

*"I told him, 'I care about you, and I'm proud of you for
going to war, but I want to teach. I'm a good teacher.*

*"He said I should just forget it. He said he was the only
person that I needed to take care of now. So, what was I going to
do? Just walk out on him? He made me feel guilty for wanting to
do what made me happy. And on top of all this, my mother
would have had a fit. The whole family was so proud of him for
being a hero. At the time it felt like it was* the right thing *to do."*

*Like so many women, Victoria let others direct her life.
She was overwhelmed by her sense of guilt and what she thought
was the right thing to do. For twenty-seven years, she remained
married to Tom, living by his rules and under his constant
direction. She raised their two children, worked at a drugstore to
help pay the mortgage, a job Tom approved of, since it didn't
take much of her attention.*

*On her fiftieth birthday he announced that he'd fallen in
love with his secretary. He walked out that night and never
returned. The pain and insult was immense, but it was an
opportunity. Six years later, with the grief of the divorce finally
behind her, Victoria is thrilled that she has the reins of her life
back, and that she has become the director of her own life.
A very happy single woman, she tells me that though she loved
teaching as a young woman, she now wants to be a research
librarian and she is studying to do just that.*

Questions to Ponder

• *What direction do you want to go in now? Is this a new direction? Or perhaps there's a new way to go in the direction you're already headed or once dreamed you'd be going?*
• *What do you imagine this new direction might look like?*

REMEMBERING THE DREAM

With several decades left to live, we have plenty of time to go for our dreams. More often than not, when we were teenagers our parents determined our direction. And more often than not we hated that direction. We had other dreams, other ideas for our futures. They may not yet have been very well thought out. They may even have been downright silly, fanciful, overly glamorous, or completely impractical. We may have followed the direction of those dreams to some extent, and we may or may not have found some degree of success. The important thing right now is to remember that we did have dreams—big dreams.

The first step is to recognize that they existed. You can do this by writing about the loss in your journal, and then giving it over to the light in your meditation.

The next step is to mourn the loss and allow the essence of the adolescent dreams to seep gently into your Power Woman consciousness by continuing to read the essays and work with the tools, games, and exercises. The direction for our Power Woman life is in the dreams and daydreams of our teenage self. The seed is there, have no doubt. It has been germinating for thirty or forty years.

My mother-in-law, Betty, is a perfect example of a woman in midlife who rediscovered the dreams of her youth. When she was fifty, her two best friends helped her to listen to her inner-voice. As a young woman she'd left college after just one year to marry my husband's father. For the next thirty years, she pushed her dreams aside and raised three children and worked at low-paying jobs to help supplement the family's income.

But finally, at fifty, she went back to school. She had to continue working full-time, so it took her awhile, but at fifty-nine she graduated with a BA in psychology. The day she walked across that stage to receive her diploma she was beaming. I don't think I'd ever seen a prouder or happier person.

Ten years later she uses her degree to work as a peer counselor with women in her community, and she tells me that it's the most rewarding thing she's ever done.

Questions to Ponder

- *Who do you look to for guidance in your life?*
- *Do you have any role models within your circle of friends and family?*

WHEREVER YOU ARE IS A STEP IN THE RIGHT DIRECTION

"Faith and doubt, both are needed, not as antagonists but working side by side, to take us around the unknown curve."

– Lillian Smith

What do you want to do for the rest of your life? This is a heady thought, isn't it? Where does one start to look for the answer to this question?

It's simple really. Start right where you are. Your Spirit knows that you are exactly where you need to be to take the next step toward your new life. Therefore it is time to listen to your Spirit. Unfortunately, few people know how to do this. Spirit's job is to guide and nudge us toward our life's purpose, and it is when we don't heed the messages of our Spirit that we experience frustration and what we often think of as failure.

One's purpose is different from one's goals. And our purpose may be very different from what we've always thought we desired for our lives. In disconnecting from old beliefs, we learn to pay attention to signs and signals, and learn the fine art of listening to Spirit.

We are all sensitive. We all have the ability to sense beyond what is obvious. Another word for this kind of sensitivity is intuition. Everyone has the facility of intuition. Some people are more naturally adept than others, but intuition develops with training. Women have always been known for their intuitive abilities. Intuition is a formidable talent, but in our male-dominated society it is not valued because it is a predominantly feminine talent. I don't mean to say that men can't be intuitive. They certainly can, and in the next fifty years we will begin to see a great majority of men working to develop their feminine sides. Their own intuitive powers will become increasingly evident to them. For now, however, we'll focus on ourselves, for we already have a pretty good handle on this sensing ability.

Developing your intuition will help you to hear the directions of your Spirit. To begin this process you must focus. Focus and direction are an inseparable duo.

Alaya, fifty-five, has been studying on a spiritual path for thirty years. Her teacher taught her how to develop her ability to listen to her Spirit. "He taught me to listen clearly within for guidance and encouraged me to NOT listen to anyone else, even him, if it was counter to my own inner guidance."

Leslie, fifty-three, a writer, says, "I think I listen, but I don't trust myself much, and I don't know what I sound like...I don't think I'm a very good thinker or visionary." Her books tell a different story. When she writes, I'm sure she listens. Yet like so many women who were abused, emotionally and/or physically by the women who raised them, Leslie doesn't trust her Spirit. In her younger years she was a journalist, but now she's begun writing fiction and it is through her fiction that her inner voice speaks.

Joyce, fifty-seven, said, "I try to listen, but my inner voice is often unsure. It seems to always be searching."

Betty, sixty-nine, says, "I listen to my inner voice, and find that I can hear it more clearly as I grow older. It comes to me in the form of feelings, either positive or negative, and I have learned to recognize and act on those feelings in the last twenty years."

Often we get clues about our purpose from the things we observe happening in the world that make us uncomfortable, where we see a need for change, and where we think we might have some ideas to help that change. Observe the things in your community or in the country or in the world that make you cringe. What are they? Why do they upset you? What could you do to help?

*Jennifer Heath is a good friend, a gifted writer, and a woman who fol-
lows her own direction. Jennifer spent her adolescence in Afghanistan where
her father was an American diplomat. As a teenager she fell in love with the
Afghan culture and the people, and gained a great deal of understanding and
respect for their Muslim faith. In midlife, she found herself writing about
Afghanistan, in her wonderful novel* A House White with Sorrow.
*She volunteered with several humanitarian efforts to help the Afghan people
rebuild their country after years of war.*

*After September 11, 2001, Jennifer began to listen to her Spirit. As she
did, she realized that although the large organizations she was involved with
had good intentions, they were also bogged down with the red tape that
plagues all large quasi-governmental agencies. But what could she do alone?
There must be something positive that she could do outside the system. She
remembered the Afghanistan of her adolescence, an exquisite, mountainous
country with gardens everywhere. But now, after decades of constant war,
Afghanistan had become a parched, barren desert.*

*And then it dawned on her. She needed to help replant the gardens. There
needed to be plants for food to feed the people, for vegetation to stop erosion,
and for beauty to help heal the souls of the people. She followed her own lead,
not the direction of agencies or institutions. She put a notice in her local
newspaper that she was collecting seeds for Afghanistan in a box on her front
porch. Anyone was welcome to donate.*

*As of this writing, she has collected more than one million packets of
seeds. She has sent them all to Afghanistan, and they have all been planted.
Through this simple project, gardens are blooming, food is being harvested,
and erosion is being stopped. Jennifer got clues from the memories of her
adolescent self, and allowed those clues to guide her in the direction that
eventually helped make a simple but positive change in the world.*

We all have good ideas. We all have feelings, aspirations, memories, and desires from our adolescent years that still have the power to motivate us, if we let them. We all have a Spirit guiding us to listen to our hearts and follow our inner direction to make changes in our lives, in our communities and in our world. Women have the answers.

Questions to Ponder

- *Who or what takes your attention away from yourself and your dreams most often?*
- *Who do you want to be the director of your life?*
- *Can you remember a time when you followed the direction of your inner voice? What was the outcome?*
- *What are some changes you'd like to see? Do you have some idea about facilitating those changes?*

THE CHALLENGE TO FOCUS ON OURSELVES

I am currently working with Laura, a businesswoman who has just sent the second of her two children off to college and is looking for her next step. She's well aware that she has a next step, but when she couldn't get a clear handle on what it was, she came to work with me. I work intuitively with my clients. I have developed the ability to listen to my client's Spirit selves and then translate what I hear back to them.

Listening to Laura's Spirit, I immediately heard, or sensed, her lack of "focus." It was clear within the first ten minutes of our first session that this was indeed Laura's challenge. Every subject we discussed started out being focused on her, but within seconds she veered away to talk about her husband or her children or people she deals with in business.

When I pointed this out, she laughed. How could she learn to focus on her next step if she couldn't focus on herself for more than a few seconds? Many women are unable to keep their minds on themselves. Our focus has been fragmented for our entire lives from necessity. As wives, mothers, and career women we learned to think of twenty things at once, or move in "toutes directions," as the signs in France say. We had to. People depended on us to know what homework needed to be done, what groceries needed to be bought, what appointments had to be kept, and what the client, the boss, and/or the employees needed. Some women were able to develop the ability to compartmentalize and focus on one thing at a time. For most women, compartmentalizing isn't the norm.

Men, on the other hand, don't seem to have this natural facility for multiple tasking. They are taught from an early age to focus on their own goals and direction, one thing at a time. This is a skill most women must learn. And when that one focus is herself, many women have an even more difficult time.

Questions to Ponder

- *Has there ever been a time when you asked a man for help in attaining your dream?*
- *Did you get the help you needed? If you did, were there any trade-offs?*

INANNA'S RETURN TO EARTH

When we left Inanna she was in the underworld, where her dark sister, Ereshkigal, Goddess of Death, had killed her and left her hanging on a meat hook to rot. On Earth, Inanna's assistant, Ninshubur, realizes that the time has come to follow Inanna's instructions and find help to get her back. She first goes to Enlil, the highest god of sky and Earth, but he turns her down. Next she goes to Inanna's father, Nanna, God of the Moon, and again her request is refused. Both of these male gods turn their backs on Inanna, because they believe they cannot interfere in the rules of the underworld. They are the patriarchs, and the most important rules of the patriarchy are law, obedience, and order. They cannot bend the law even for the Great Goddess or for the Earth, where the land lies barren and the people are starving. The story shows us that, more often than not, when times are roughest, women turn to the men in their lives. We may even find ourselves asking permission from the male figures in our lives before we feel free to move in our own direction.

Ninshubur gets no help from the first two gods on her list. Next, she goes to Enki, God of Water and Wisdom. Although he was considered fundamentally a male god, Enki was also thought to be of both sexes, having in one myth undergone an "eight-fold pregnancy." And it is this more ebullient, transsexual god who finally enables Inanna's escape. He creates two little creatures, neither male nor female, from the dirt under his red–painted fingernails. These creatures are so insignificant they are able to sneak past the guards and release Inanna.

There is something fascinating about Enki and these little creatures and their ability to help Inanna in her ascent back to earth. As was discussed earlier, Inanna's descent to visit the dark goddess Ereshkigal, and Inanna's subsequent death, represent the descent women take into the death of our childbearing ability during menopause. When we get to the place in our menopausal journey where all seems darkness and death, and rebirth is an impossible concept to imagine, something inside begins to tickle at us. Some sense of new life pricks at our exhausted hearts, and slowly we see signs of life. There's a light at the end of the tunnel, and it comes from the watery depths of our emotions, symbolized in the Inanna myth by the water god Enki. The light becomes stronger and more powerful until we finally burst up out of the darkness and are reborn as a brand-new woman.

The little creatures, having awakened Inanna, led her up through the many levels of the underworld. At each gate she was reinvested with a garment of the new woman she was birthing. At the first level, she was fitted with under garments of fine silks to protect the fragile body that was just beginning to come back to life. At the second level of her ascent, she was dressed in a gown embroidered with threads of her newly emerging radiance. And it is here that she was awakened enough to realize that she was indeed alive once more.

Energized by this new awareness, Inanna eagerly rises to the third level and accepts a necklace set with all the gemstones of the world.

When she enters the fourth level she remarks that death has left her feeling vulnerable. The guardian wraps a cape of protection around her shoulders and sends her on to the fifth level, where she is presented with a crown of emeralds, reminding her of the beauty of the green fields in the land she had been away from for so long.

As she approaches the sixth level, Inanna wonders if she will be remembered by anyone on Earth after such a long absence. To assuage her fears, she is given a great staff that carries her seal. Fully clothed, her crown set firmly on her head, her staff in hand, she steps confidently into the seventh and final level and immediately burns her feet on hot coals. This reminds her that she is not quite ready to take that final step onto the Earth. She sits down and as the shoemakers mold gold-and-silver sandals to the perfect shape of her feet, she contemplates all she has been through. She remembers the younger goddess she was when she entered the underworld alone to spend eternity with her dear sister Ereshkigal. She feels the pain and darkness of her time on the meat hook and she marvels at her strength to bear it.

Finally, her new sandals finished and fastened around her ankles, she is ready to leave this place of death and transformation. The gates are flung open and Inanna steps into the world. It is a new world, one with which she is not familiar. It is not the world that has changed, but she who is not the same. She has been into the heart of darkness, she has died, and she has been reborn. No longer is she the goddess always ready to do her father or husband's bidding to keep peace in their kingdoms. Now, she is a ruthless, powerful female, who claims her right to survive, thrive, and bring change to the Earth.

It may surprise you to learn, as it did me, that we know so much about Inanna because the earliest identified work in all of world literature was written about her by a woman named Enheduanna, the high priestess of Inanna in Sumeria (present-day Iraq) around 2300 BCE. When Enheduanna tells us about Inanna's return from the dead she declares that Inanna has become the most powerful being in the universe. She tells us that what was once spoken of her father, Nanna, King of the Gods, is now said of his daughter. Inanna is as lofty as heaven, she tells us, and it must be known throughout the world that Inanna devastates the rebellious, roars at the land, rains blows on the heads of those who do not revere her, and feasts on their corpses like a dog. Inanna's mere glance is like a strike of lightning, and Inanna, above all the gods, is the High and Holy One.

As we work with our own new direction, we can think of ourselves moving up through the levels of the underworld, regaining, one by one, our garments of power. At each level of our ascent, we will seek clues to what our direction will be. We will learn to hear the words of our own Enki spirit, the emotional wisdom that is not guided by intellectual rules of order or the laws of gender, but by the heart's wisdom. At last, arriving at the entrance to the sun-filled world, we stand ready to step out in a brand-new direction.

Filled with this new awesome power, we stand befuddled, just awakening to the possibilities. This is a new kind of feminine power. Power that must be taken. No one will give it to us. It is too extraordinary, too outlandish, and too downright scary for even our closest family members to embrace completely. We will have to teach them slowly. But we can't wait for them to understand it. We alone must grapple with it. Find our direction. Find women to support our direction, and make the necessary steps to secure our footing on this new path. Then, once on solid ground, we can take time to coax those close to us into accepting our new direction.

Questions to Ponder

- *Do you listen to your own inner voice when you're looking for direction?*
- *If you do, how do you hear it? If you don't, what is stopping you?*

PAYING ATTENTION

To find your direction, you must learn to listen to the inner voice of your Spirit. To do this, you will need to expand your awareness of the larger world while simultaneously turning inward to become aware of your own feelings, thoughts, and sensations. Your Spirit speaks to you in many ways, from gut feelings to external signs. By paying attention to everything around you, as well as your feelings and instincts, you will begin to recognize subtle but very real messages.

To begin, it is helpful to become more conscious of where you are and what you're experiencing at any given moment. That means becoming aware of what is going on around you, as well as inside you. What color are the flowers in the pot on the porch? What is the woman across the aisle wearing? What does your own voice sound like when you're talking on the phone with your husband, partner, girlfriend, or mother? What part of your body tenses up when an angry neighbor accosts you with another petty complaint?

It is important to become aware of your surroundings and your own feelings and sensations because they are all part of an integrated whole – and it is in this wholeness that the messages from your spirit lie. It is also helpful to know which feelings belong to you and which are sensations you may be picking up from others around you. Although extra-sensory perception is regarded as the domain of psychics, all sensitive human beings are able to sense another person's feelings.

During an ordinary day you may find yourself feeling fearful or angry. Your immediate reaction is probably to ignore or repress these feelings. But now that you are consciously working to hear your inner voice, you need to acknowledge all feelings. Ask yourself, what is making you angry or frightened? If you can't find an answer, you may very well be picking up the anger or fear from someone you are standing near, or who has just walked past you. By learning to differentiate between your own feelings and those of others around you, you begin to eliminate unnecessary input that interrupts the signals from your inner voice.

Trying to pay attention to all these things at once may be a bit overwhelming at first. Just take it one step at a time. Let's start with something simple and very practical. While you're driving the car, pay attention to the fact that you're driving. For most people driving has become a habit with very little conscious focus. As you drive, become aware of the cars next to you. What color are they? What kind of shape are they in? Look at the red light and make a conscious note of the fact that you are stopped at the red light. Look at the woman in the car next to you or ahead of you. Does she have her mind on the road, is she putting on make-up, talking on the phone, yelling at her kids? Look at your dashboard. Are there any lights lit up that shouldn't be? Listen to the engine. Does it sound like it's in good running condition? Though these all seem like logical things to pay attention to, few of us do. We get in the car and put it on autopilot. Most accidents would be avoided if drivers paid attention. Every time you get into your car from now on, make a conscious effort to pay attention.

How does driving your car apply to hearing your spirit and ulti-mately deciphering your life's direction? First of all, when you become aware of what is going on in the world around you, over time you notice when something is different than usual. That difference may be a subtle signal alerting you to something important. You will also be putting your focus on your life at that moment. Being in the moment is being at peace. In the moment all is well. There is no worry about the future or guilt from the past. You simply are. From this point of peace you are able to follow subtle clues directing you to take your next incremental step.

I'll give you an example of this theory in action. One afternoon several years ago I got in my car heading for the supermarket. Within a block, I had moved into my normal spaced-out mode. Suddenly I found myself ten blocks past the market. The traffic was bad, and it took me twenty minutes to get back to the store. By the time I arrived, I was becoming irritable. On top of everything else, the store had run out of cooked chickens, which I was really counting on for dinner. I had to think of something else, and that took time I didn't have. The more I searched the store for something to cook, the more frustrated I became. I ended up snapping at the clerk and stumbling over a basket on my way out of the store. By the time I got home I was exhausted and angry.

Unfortunately, this is how many of us live a good portion of our lives. But what if I had been paying attention?

Let's consider a similar scenario, with you, or someone not unlike you, as the heroine. It's a crisp fall afternoon. You get into your car heading for the supermarket. You are aware and alert. Ahead you see that cars are starting to put on their brakes; a traffic jam seems likely. You remember a shortcut. You turn off the busy street and get to the store in better time than usual. You go to the cooked chicken counter, pick up one of the last chickens. With time to spare you wander over to the bakery. While perusing the pies, someone you haven't seen for several years walks up. She's very pleased to see you. She remembers that you have a background in finance. You cringe because you left the corporate world with glee on your forty-fifth birthday, so that you could pursue something altruistic. You refrain from saying anything. Then she explains that she's looking for a woman to facilitate the distribution of micro-finance loans for poverty-level women to create home-based businesses. Within days you are on a plane to Bangladesh to train for your new career. Although you left the corporate finance world, your background gives you a great advantage for your new career. You have always dreamed of traveling to remote places in the world. Now you are being paid for it, and fulfilling your desire to facilitate positive change in the world.

Carl Jung calls this synchronicity, the universe conspiring to get us where our Spirit selves know we should be. When we become alert and aware, we can't help but take the next step in the right direction.

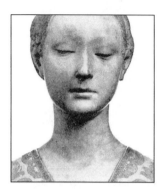

LISTENING TO THE VOICE OF YOUR SPIRIT

"Although I try
to hold the single thought
of Buddha's teaching in my heart,
I cannot help but hear
the many crickets' voices calling as well."

– Izumi Shikibu (974 – 1034 CE)

Spirit's voice is talking to us all the time. But usually the din of all the other voices that fill our minds blocks this beautiful voice of our true nature. Some of these voices are the cries of fear, grief, and anger, which we've stored over a lifetime. Other voices are what I call "blathering." They are the whining, the griping, the gossiping, and all the other kinds of mindless chatter. Using journaling and meditation, we are little by little hearing the cries for help. By finding self-love and self-trust, the mindless chatter will begin to lessen. Over a period of time, our true selves will prevail, and we will tear away the veil that separates us from our Spirit. We will start to hear, feel, or sense what our Spirit wants us to do. We will begin to understand intuitively that following one route and not another will lead us to a place that is in line with our Spirit's will for us as we take one more giant step into our Power Women selves.

GAMES AND EXERCISES

WEEK SEVEN: THE POWER OF OUR OWN DIRECTION

1. Make a list of twenty things you like to do. They can be any kind of things—skating, sleeping, knitting, rock-climbing, daydreaming—anything that you like to do.

2. Take a half-hour walk and try to be conscious and aware during the entire walk. Notice the color of the sky, the sound of the wind in the leaves, the animals, insects, smells, other people, and even begin to notice if you can sense how the person who has just walked past you is feeling.

3. Look into the life of your role-model and see if there are any clues in her teen years that led to the direction she took in her older life.

4. This is a two-parter:
   a. While looking at the photo of your teenage self, write a letter to her. Tell her what you're doing now. Ask her if she is happy with how your life has gone so far. Ask her what she would have done differently.

   b. Write a letter from your teenage self to your mid-life self. Respond to the previous letter and add anything else that your teenage self feels like saying to you mid-life self.

5. Spend time working on your report on your role model, so that you can be ready to share it with your circle at your next meeting.

REMEMBER to journal and meditate daily. Ask your teenage self to help you find your true direction as you journal. Spend more time with your teenage self in your Sacred Room during your meditations. Tell her how much you appreciate her and her dreams.

THE POWER OF

Partnership & Community

"Know the strength of man, but keep a woman's care!
Be the stream of the universe."

– Tao Te Ching

On the next leg of the journey, many emerging Power Women may experience conflicting emotions. Working and playing in community — especially with other women—is our natural state, and comes from our cellular memory of ancient ancestors sitting together in red tents and moon huts, creating a synergy of feminine power to use constructively for the good of the tribes.

But having been trained as enemies over the past few millennia, we now often find ourselves simultaneously yearning and shying away from the community of women. Yet we are most authentic working with other women. We love gathering in circles to tell each other our stories. In recent history, women have come together to make quilts, or tear bandages for war efforts, or organize church socials. Today, many women are joining simply to rediscover the pleasure of each other's company. When women sit together, we chat. And when women chat, we can, once we move from gossip to more serious concerns, come up with inspired solutions to problems facing our communities and us. We learn best when we are gathered together and share what we know.

Women formed the original communities and we also make great partners. We understand innately how to share. We know what it means to take a front seat at times and a back seat at others. Unfortunately, when it comes to relationships with men, we have not had enough opportunity to be equal partners. Recently, however, more and more men are softening to the idea and many are actively working on becoming more loving and generous partners. The trick to meeting an equal partner or helping our current partners become more equal is finding our own inner balance.

Questions to Ponder

- *Have you ever felt frustrated or angry about not being considered an equal partner?*
- *Do you like to work in a communal atmosphere? Why? Or, why not?*
- *If you have a life partner now, is there anything you would change in your relationship?*

THE YIN AND THE YANG OF IT

To become partners in truly balanced relationships, whether love, business or others of life's endeavors, we must develop a balanced and harmonious relationship within our own nature. As women, we have been harmed greatly by the servile role we have been forced to play throughout history. Though we have made great steps in the past century and especially during the last thirty-five years, we still have much to heal within society and ourselves.

Each of us has both a feminine and a masculine side. As you've learned by working with the Yin-Yang Energy Meditation, these two forces work on the magnetic and dynamic principles that, when given the chance, dance together in amazing balance and harmony. As we learn to love both the Yin and Yang of our own personalities, we will be able to embrace both images with equal enthusiasm.

Although all people carry feminine and masculine energies, for women, the feminine nature is more fully developed in the first half of life for the simple reason that our biological purpose is to bear children. But as we move out of the childbearing years, we have the opportunity to develop our masculine natures more fully, so that we can stand more equally balanced within ourselves.

DISCOVERING OUR MASCULINE/DYNAMIC SIDE

I began having hot flashes when I turned forty. My first were in a chateau in northern France. I was coming to the end of a year spent working and living in Europe and doing a little traveling with my closest friend. We were having dinner in the dining room when sweat started pouring from my scalp and dripping onto the white linen tablecloth. I glanced around and wondered why no one else in the room seemed to notice the extreme heat. I was wearing a new wool-knit dress I'd bought in Milan. At first I thought that was the problem, but as I glanced around the room, I saw that everyone else wore cold-weather clothes, too. My friend was obviously becoming embarrassed.

The intensity of the heat finally drove me out of my chair. I ran upstairs to our room, flung open the doors to the terrace, and tore off all my clothes. The cold October wind blew against my steaming, naked body and then, as quickly as it started, it was over. In that moment of relief, I realized I'd had a hot flash.

My friend was shocked when I returned to the dining room and told her. Neither of us had been taught anything about menopause or hot flashes. Her mother died when she was eight, and my mother denied ever having experienced it. This was in the mid-eighties and peri-menopause was just being identified as an early stage of hormonal change, and I was in it. There I was, returning home to Los Angeles at forty with hot flashes. After an exciting year in Europe, I'd assumed I would be re-entering my normal life. Little did I know that these "power surges" were incubating a whole new me. I had crossed a threshold into a special world where I would experience a series of revelations that would keep me occupied for more than a decade and deliver up a different woman on the other side of fifty.

My first adventure on this side of the threshold was the discovery of my masculine, or Yang, energy. One of my last stops in Europe was London, where I saw the musical *Cats*. The character of the Rock and Roll Cat fascinated me. I couldn't get him out of my mind. This *cat* was a very sexy, male cat, who played in a rock band, and had all the characteristics of a rock star: self-assured, swaggering, a seductive rogue. He appeared in my daydreams and my sleeping dreams. I was single, so I just assumed this was some necessary fantasy to get me through a time without a boyfriend. But what it turned out to be was far more interesting.

I was still enamored with the Rock and Roll Cat, when I saw a concert movie, *Bring on the Night*, featuring Sting and his band. Most of the film was shot in a chateau outside Paris, reminiscent of the location of my first hot flash. That night, the Rock and Roll Cat disappeared from my dreams and Sting took his place. I saw the movie five times. I took all my girlfriends to see it. I began to obsess over the movie and its star. When I grasped that I was falling in love with Sting, I was more than a little embarrassed. I hadn't had this kind of intense feeling for a celebrity since adolescence. Working in theatre and the film industry most of my life, I knew too much about stars to be seduced by them. But suddenly there I was, a forty-year-old, peri-menopausal woman head-over-heels for a rock star. Then the ultimate happened, my neighbor got me a pirated copy of the video. Once I had Sting in my apartment alone, I had to look deeply at what was really going on with me, and what I discovered was amazing.

One evening, while sipping a glass of excellent chardonnay and watching *Bring on the Night* for probably the tenth time, it occurred to me: Sting and the Rock and Roll Cat had captured my heart, because they were reflections of my own newly developing masculine energy. I wasn't in love with a rock star. I was in love with my young, vibrant, emergent, inner male self.

Before I go further I want to make it clear that the development of a woman's inner masculine self, is not the same as imitating men, which so many of us did and do in the world of business. Rather, it is about opening to that vigorous Yang (which translated is "flags flying in the sun") part of our personalities cupped in the grail of our feminine bodies and consciousness. As I learned in retrospect, my feelings about Sting were not about Sting per se, but only the Sting as portrayed in this particular documentary. The first two-thirds of the film follows Sting and his band as they rehearse, get to know each other, and create new songs, new arrangements, and new relationships. It shows the beauty of artists working in community to create a particular piece of art, in this case a record album. As a young person, I had been drawn to the worlds of the theatre and film-making because of the communal creative process. And now, as I was developing my new female/male inner partnership I was rediscovering the joy of communal creative endeavors.

In the film's final act, at the end of the band's first concert performance, Sting's partner, Trudie Styler, goes into labor. We watch Trudie giving birth, Sting at her side, his voice in the background singing "I Hope the Russians Love Their Children Too." This was 1985 and a film with a man in a delivery room was still relatively unusual.

For me, the film's most powerful moment comes as Sting is being interviewed off-screen about the delivery while we watch the baby taken from Trudie's womb and laid on her tummy. "It's easy to come in after the fact, and they're all clean in their white nightgowns and their hair brushed," Sting tells the interviewer. "The reality is much more bloody and profound."

"Much more bloody and profound." That line opened a whole new world for me. Here was a male rock star talking about the profundity of blood. The whole messy stuff about menstruating (the "curse") and birth, which I had been raised to believe was shameful, was suddenly elevated to a place of reverence. "Much more bloody and profound." There and then, my understanding of the world, history, and women was turned upside-down. I've been dedicated to expressing the profundity of feminine blood ever since.

In the process of discovering my masculine Yang energy, I was concurrently gaining a deeper appreciation of my feminine Yin energy. In retrospect, I recognize that the birth of Sting's son was also a foreshadowing of the birth of my new self.

Once I understood what was happening I could begin to explore a love affair with myself. I meditated on it daily, and allowed myself to give up to the turbulent feelings that churned inside of me. It was a luscious time. My affair with Sting and the film, or more correctly, with myself, lasted for almost two years. During that time I had no dates with anyone else, and I was beginning to think I'd never have another date. The truth is that there was no room for another person. My relationship with myself was all consuming.

Gradually I stopped thinking about Sting altogether and became aware instead of a serene balance trickling, then flowing, through me. I walked a little differently. I stood taller. I spoke with more self-assurance, and I was generally a more balanced human being.

Questions to Ponder

- *What was your first experience with hot flashes?*
- *Is there one particular male celebrity who touches your heart?*
- *Do you spend time being intimate with yourself?*

A ROOM OF ONE'S OWN

In her 1928 book, *A Room of One's Own*, Virginia Woolf makes a strong case for every woman writer having a room of her own and five hundred pounds a year, which translates to about fifty thousand dollars today. I'm all for it, and I don't believe that this applies only to writers. Every woman is a creative being, and the more she nurtures that creative seed within her, the healthier, happier, and more whole she becomes.

Having a room of one's own is extremely nurturing. The majority of women spend most waking and sleeping hours in the presence of others. Few of us have a place that is just ours, a place where we can close the door to the desires and needs of others. It has never even occurred to the majority of women that this is something we should or could have. Men have their dens. Children have their playrooms, and families have their family rooms. Nowadays with increasing numbers of people working at home, there are home offices, but few of these spaces belong specifically to women. More often than not these are shared quarters for the purpose of making money and taking care of family finances.

A room of one's own is a place that is specifically yours. It cannot be entered by anyone unless by invitation. It can be messy or neat—no one will notice or care but you. You can work, play, paint, write, sew, or just lie around in your room. You can discover the Yin and Yang within yourself and begin to balance them alone in your room. You can throw off the day's responsibilities and think only of yourself, your dreams, and your desires. You can watch movies, drink tea, sprawl naked on the floor. You can read a good book propped up on pillows in a cozy corner. You can have an affair with yourself alone in your room.

The two years that I spent in love with Sting/myself, I was lucky enough to have an apartment that was just mine. I was single and my son was on his own for the first time. I indulged myself. I wrote, I cried, and I dressed in sexy lingerie to watch my Sting movie over and over again. I explored myself in every imaginable way. I gave myself the complete freedom to do it. I learned what few women in our generation and society know. I learned to become intimate with myself. And I grew! I changed! I, who had been what one might consider an interesting younger woman, became—to myself—a remarkable older woman.

Find a space in your house that can become your own room. Take it. Don't ask if anyone minds. Simply announce firmly that it's yours. Then move in. It may be only a large closet you recreate as a cozy nook, but whatever the size, take it and make it your own.

Once you have created your room, spend time in it everyday. At first, it may take some discipline to spend time alone. Discovering ourselves can be frightening. It's often much easier to keep occupied with others' problems, wants, and needs. But go for it. Be courageous. It is with this kind of courage that you will discover your Yang self.

Questions to Ponder

- *How much of each day do you spend alone doing exactly what you want to do?*
- *What do you do when you're alone? Do you get bored?*
- *Did you have a room of your own when you were a child? If not, did you have a special place where you could be alone?*
- *What would the ultimate room of your own be like?*

ARTHUR AND GUINEVERE

Most women either openly or secretly dream of a peaceful, harmonious society. And most mid-life emerging Power Women have been working toward that end in some way or other for much of our lives, whether protesting the war in Viet Nam, participating in the Civil Rights Movement, working for the rights of women and children, or for the environment. Although most of us consider a utopian world just a fantastic dream, this doesn't stop us from longing for it. And it hasn't stopped many of us from actively working toward it.

When I can't imagine something happening in the future, I look to the past, either historical or mythical, to find examples. If someone has done it before, it gives me hope that it can happen again. Our culture's most beloved myth is of the beautifully balanced partnership of Arthur and Guinivere.

Geoffrey of Monmouth first wrote about the legend of Camelot in the twelfth century. Among the most famous versions of the tale are Tennyson's *Idylls of the King* and Mallory's *Mort d'Arthur*, though today's readers are perhaps most familiar with Mary Stewart's *Merlin Trilogy* and T.H. White's *The Once and Future King*.

White's book became the basis for Lerner and Lowe's Broadway musical *Camelot*, and it was during its Broadway run that the United States was swathed in an Arthurian romance of its own, with Jack and Jackie Kennedy, our Arthur and Guinevere. The play opened at New York's Majestic Theatre on December 3, 1960, one month after Kennedy's election as president, and closed January 5, 1963, a little less than two months after his assassination.

King Arthur, like President John F. Kennedy, was beloved by all, and yet there were forces conspiring to kill them both. Forty years after his assassination, we who were alive at the time cannot forget the magic of those Camelot years. King Arthur is said to have been taken by the Great Goddess back to the Isle of Avalon to await a time in the future when the world was ready for his gift as a mature leader and loving partner, and many people today still hold the memory of John Fitzgerald Kennedy in their hearts with the same hope.

The mythic Camelot is a land where peace has come after decades of war and tyrannical leaders. A kind, just, and honest youth comes to the throne after being given the sword of truth, "Excalibur," by the Lady of the Lake, the Great Goddess. To further help the young Arthur bring peace to his land, the Goddess sends him her handmaiden, Guinevere, to be his queen. Guinevere brings her new husband the third gift of the Goddess, the Round Table, where all are equal, since there is no head of a round table. In mythic terms this is the gift of sitting in circle that all women knew in ancient times.

As we sit in circle now, we can begin to see how we might bring that gift to our own society.

Wendy, fifty, a freelance graphic designer, talked to me about joining a social club in high school that wouldn't accept her best friend Nancy. Though it was difficult for Wendy to turn her back on her friend, acceptance by the social club was more important to her at the time. When I asked her if she felt sorry about it now, she said, "of course." I suggested that she try to find Nancy and reconnect. She did. They met for coffee and found that they had a lot in common. Wendy told me that it was difficult to apologize, but when she finally did it, she felt wonderful, and Nancy appreciated it a great deal.

BEST FRIENDS FOR LIFE

As little girls most of us had a best friend, someone who we became blood sisters with, went to camp with, and sold lemonade in the front yard with. When we became teenagers sometimes we kept that same best friend, but sometimes the circumstances of adolescence were such that we lost our best friend.

When little girls move into adolescence, society traps us with its false values and inability to accept or acknowledge feminine power. In one way or another we succumb to the pressures. Had we been taken into the red tent at thirteen, we would have learned to value each other by the example set by our mothers and grandmothers. Unfortunately, we have had no such luxury.

But even as we blundered through adolescence, most of us did find friends with whom we could bond. Most of us had at least a small band of girlfriends. And when we remember the nights waiting for the boys to call, the times we styled each other's hair, raided our parents' liquor cabinets, or sat up all night reading the dirty parts of *Peyton Place, Sex and the Single Girl,* or *Fear of Flying,* we get a particularly warm feeling in our hearts. There's something about the community of girls and women that fills a place within us that our relationships with boys and men can never fill.

Ginny, a fifty-one-year-old greeting card designer, told me about a New Year's Eve when she was sixteen. She lived with her single mother and older brother. Both her mom and brother were going out, but Ginny didn't have a date. Luckily, neither did her two closest friends. The three girls decided to spend the evening together at her house.

"We were kind of geeks. We didn't have many dates, so it was okay to spend the afternoon and early evening styling each other's hair, trying on fancy clothes, and making brownies—the legal kind. We had a ball. When my mother and brother left, we raided the liquor cabinet and made frozen daiquiris. After we got a little tipsy, we got brave enough to call up a boy that my friend Bonnie liked."

To their surprise he was home with two friends. The boys joined the girls and they had, in Ginny's words, "one hell of a night."

The most vivid part of Ginny's story was about the early evening before the boys got there. When I mentioned this, she said, "Yes, the best part of that New Year's Eve was the prepara-tion, the time when we girls just played together. I particularly remember the three of us trying to find a recipe for the daiquiris and the fun we had mixing the ingredients and tasting."

I recently reconnected with my best childhood friend, Buffy. We were inseparable from the third grade until adolescence, when the more popular girls were able to woo her away from me, and soon after that, she moved to another town. She had been so dear to me when I was a little girl that I never stopped loving her. When we got together on the phone forty years later, it was as though we had never been apart. We laughed and giggled, and told stories. She also told me that she had suffered a brain tumor and was recovering from cancer. I was so glad I had made the call.

Then she suggested we get some of the girls from our old Brownie troop together for a reunion. At first, I resisted the idea. I wanted to see Buffy more than anything, but I wasn't sure about the others. Some had been less than kind to me during junior high and high school. I wasn't a girl who fit into cliques, and I still carried the wounds of that teenage rejection.

I hemmed and hawed, but Buffy insisted that I come. She set the date around my schedule, so I finally had to give in. For the four weeks leading up to the reunion, I journaled daily about my old adolescent hurts. I wrote about how much I didn't want to go to see these women, and even fantasized hideous hurtful things they would say to me. It wasn't rational. It was the pain of adolescence that I'd never processed. Even with all my journaling and meditating, I was still a bit on edge when I boarded the plane for San Francisco.

The plan was to spend the weekend at Susie's house in the wine country north of San Francisco. I picked Buffy up at her house in Marin County. She was beautiful. Blonde braids, and a patch over one eye that had been damaged by the brain tumor and surgery. It felt so wonderful to be with her. We laughed and talked non-stop on the hour drive to Susie's house. Susie welcomed us with open arms. The three of us cooked dinner and reminisced. A couple of hours later, Bonnie arrived. The four of us sat up in our pajamas and chatted. So far, so good. In the morning six more showed up. We were ten women, who together had made picture frames out of bottle tops, painted ceramic George and Martha Washingtons, and saved half-drowned kittens at day camp.

We looked older, and yet we looked the same. Kathy had the same sly twinkle in her eye she had when she was six. Marsha was still precious. Cindy had the same thin lips and pretty nose. Vicki was there without her twin Micki. Her hair was white, but her dark brown eyes sparkled. Carolyn and Ellen rounded out the group, both looking like the girls they had been. I realized I wasn't the only nervous one there. Though we were all mature women who had lived full lives, there was an anxious little girl in every one of us.

On Saturday morning we gathered around a large table in Susie's sun-dappled garden and decided to begin by telling a little about our lives over the past forty years. It seemed like something we could do in a couple of hours. It ended up taking a day and a half. Summarizing doesn't seem like an option when you're talking to women who knew you when you started kindergarten.

I was having the time of my life. These weren't new friends with whom I was sharing a few stories. These were the sisters of my original tribe. Each woman told her story, and every other woman listened with full attention. Every woman's story deserved to be held and honored. When we heard the stories of success we rejoiced. When we heard the stories of tragedy and loss, we expressed our compassion. When the stories of current struggles were shared we offered help and support.

By the end of the weekend, I felt swathed in love. The women I remembered as mean girls had grown into loving, nurturing, caring people. The wounds I had nursed for decades healed in the embrace of our sisterhood. Ellen, Bonnie, Buffy, Susie, Carolyn, Cindy, Marsha, Kathy, and Vicki: thank you.

Questions to Ponder

- *Who was your best childhood friend? Did you remain best friends? If not, why?*
- *Who was your nemesis? Have you seen her lately?*
- *Did you spend more time with girls or boys as a teen?*
- *Did your parents approve of your friends?*
- *What were some of the most memorable events of your teen years?*

BEING A GOOD PARTNER

We have all had bad partners, whether they've been lovers, friends or business associates.

In my years in the movie industry, I partnered with several men and women for writing and producing. Whether or not these partnerships were good, they were all valuable in some way. I always took at least one or two good lessons away even from the bad alliances.

My love relationships were the same way: always good for my growth and development, with some good times and sweet love along the way. I have learned that it's possible and even easy to see, in retrospect, the positive in everything, once we give up our need to hold on to resentment. Resentment blocks us from allowing the essence, or the gift, of our difficult life experiences to flow into our hearts.

Having difficult partners is one thing. But what about *being* a difficult partner? We all have unique personalities, particular fears, anxieties, wishes, needs, and expectations. Like it or not, the people we partner with in love or business tend to reflect back to us, or act as mirrors to us, of our own positive, as well as negative, personality traits. It takes some courage to look at our parts in partnership problems.

Eating crow can sometimes be our best medicine. Take a moment to think back to a partnership in the past; the further back the easier it is to accept our own shortcomings. After all, we were so young, who could fault us? Were you overly needy or overly controlling? Did you want from your partner what you needed to find within yourself? So often, we discover that the qualities we're seeking in a partner are right there within ourselves. Our Spirits continuously provide us with partners who can help us finally get there—usually by making us so fed up with them that we are forced to look within.

Becoming a good partner with yourself will ultimately make you a good partner for someone else. Just before I met my husband, I was in a circle of women. Each time we met, we spent the last part of the evening telling the circle and the universe what we wanted in our lives. At that time, I was single and focused on my career. When it was my turn to tell my desire, it was always about business, and I was always very clear about how I would phrase my request to the universe.

But one night, for some reason, I didn't have anything in mind. When it was my turn, I was unprepared. Just as I was about to repeat the previous meeting's request I heard myself saying instead, "I would like to have a life partner who mirrors all the good things that I am."

I surprised myself. I didn't think I wanted a new man in my life. It hadn't occurred to me. For the first time in my life, I was truly happy being alone. I was unaware of my desire, but my Spirit knew I was ready for a wonderful partner. A week later I met my husband, Patrick. We have been together for sixteen years. And yes, he shows me daily my good qualities, as well as problems I still have to work on.

Being a good partner starts with ourselves. Once we love, respect, trust, and honor ourselves we attract the same. When we treat ourselves well, we treat others well.

WORKING IN COMMUNITY

"Community means strength that joins our strength to do the work that needs to be done."

– Starhawk

For the first half-century that movies were made, it was an accepted fact that many people worked together as a team to create a film. There were, of course, the megalomaniac studio moguls, but otherwise, everyone in the business was a working part of the whole.

Then in the 1950s, the French film director Francois Truffaut, decided that the director was the king of the film and that everyone else merely worked for his vision. They called this the Auteur Theory, and we have been stuck with it ever since.

A few years ago, one of Hollywood's few female directors was criticized by the studio chief at Twentieth Century Fox for not being assertive enough. She was observed talking to others on the set about a creative decision she had to make during a day of shooting. According to that male studio head, and the many others who agreed with him, a director should not ask others for their input or suggestions, because it gives the impression that she doesn't know what she's doing. This was perceived to be female weakness, and ultimately cost the woman her job.

Working in community is the very basis of the female process, as it is of the communal art of filmmaking. For the most part, this is true for all the arts: theatre, dance, and music. Actors, dancers, costumers, set designers, and musicians work in concert to create and present these art forms.

Ancient people danced, sang, made music, and created dramas as part of their worship. Communal ceremonies brought the tribe together with each other and the gods. Being in community, working, playing, celebrating, grieving, and praying engenders a feeling of well being in us all. Human beings are one family. A sacred tribe. It is my belief the more time we spend in loving community, the better we become as people.

Working in community is crucial for Power Women. If you work at home, you will need to find something to do outside your house with people. For many of us, working at home is preferable to working in large, stressful corporate settings. Nevertheless, we still need the company of other women and enlightened men, with whom to connect and create. Volunteering for community projects is a wonderful way to interact with others and bring our Power Women skills and ideas to the greater group.

As I stressed earlier in the "Power of True Wealth," I don't advocate volunteer work instead of paid work. But in addition to paid work, we must give to the community. Our communities need our input. I suggest that everyone volunteer at least one or two days a month and find the joy that comes from working in and for community. You may even find that while doing the volunteer work you will find the next step on your path toward your purpose. As Power Women, we can begin to create communities that can reshape our world.

Find ways to come together in community as often as you can. There is a time for solitude and a time for togetherness.

Questions to Ponder

- *What volunteer work have you done in your life?*
- *What are a few of the things you found rewarding in your previous volunteer work?*
- *What was not so rewarding?*
- *What does working in community mean to you?*
- *Do you like working with other women? If not, why not?*

GAMES AND EXERCISES

WEEK EIGHT: THE POWER OF PARTNERSHIP & COMMUNITY

1. Set your car radio on the oldies station. Sing along with every song you can.

2. Make a list of the songs from your radio listening that strike a note in your memory. Pick one song and write about the memory it elicits.

3. Create a room of your own. If you already have one, spend time decorating it or sprucing it up in some way. If you don't have enough space in your home for a whole room, create a cozy nook somewhere in the house, which you can curtain off for privacy. Make it pretty and very friendly. If you live alone, create a space that is just for special times with yourself.

4. Make a list of all the partnerships you can remember from childhood to present time. This includes girlfriends, boyfriends, lovers, husbands, and business partners.

   a. From this list, make a second list of the partnerships you felt were the most balanced. Ask yourself, what worked?

   b. Make a third list of the partnerships you felt were the most unbalanced. Ask yourself, what didn't work?

   c. Contemplate and/or write about any common threads you find as you look at these past partnerships.

5. Look for a community project where you can volunteer. Make the commitment to begin right away.

GAMES AND EXERCISES

6. Finish the report about your role model. Prepare a 5- to 10-minute talk to be presented to your circle. (Allow enough time at the circle gatherings for all the role model reports to be presented over the next three meetings. Make sure to have them all completed before the final ceremony. If you are doing this course on your own, it's time to begin writing your article or essay, and exploring where you might get it published. The Internet is a wonderful place to share stories like these.)

REMEMBER to journal and meditate daily. Are you finding that you can communicate directly with your Spirit through your journaling? In your meditations ask your Spirit to reveal herself to you in your Sacred Room.

THE POWER OF

Authentic Leadership

"Our strength is often composed of the weakness we're damned if we're going to show."

– Mignon McLaughlin

Once we have embraced the Power of Partnership and Community we are ready to take the next step into the Power of Authentic Leadership. An authentic leader must be a good partner and a champion of community. Many people have the potential for leadership, but few feel ready or able to take up the challenge that it presents. There are numerous reasons for this, and one is that women have been denied leadership roles until very recently. Also, for many women, leadership as defined by the male model of dominator-over-dominated is simply not appealing. For other women, jumping the hurdles set in the path of leadership is too daunting. Yes, more women than ever before have assumed leadership positions, which is heartening indeed, but historically, great women leaders are few and far between.

At the dawn of the new millennium it becomes increasingly apparent that a fresh kind of leadership is necessary. Great women leaders are called for now to help the world move past the conquer-and-revenge model into one of diplomacy and accord. Whether in their communities or on the world stage, women, trained by life's experience, have the potential to lead the human race into a new era.

Questions to Ponder

- *Do you desire to be a leader? If yes, why?*
- *Do you dislike the idea of taking a leadership role? If yes, why?*
- *What kind of images does the word leadership conjure in your mind?*

BOUDICCA, THE WARRIOR QUEEN

A little less than two thousand years ago and just thirty years after the death of Jesus Christ, a woman named Boudicca lived in relative peace with her husband and two teenage daughters. They were the royal family of the Celtic clan known as the Iceni, whose lands now compose the county of Norfolk, England, just northeast of London. Boudicca is remembered for having united the Celtic tribes of Britain, something no Celtic leader in

Britain had ever done. Doing so, she nearly succeeded in driving the Romans out.

The Celts, who inhabited much of Europe and the British Isles in the last millennium BCE, were a warlike people who, though seemingly ensconced in the dominator model, were still in transition from a matrilineal society or goddess society to a patriarchal society. Therefore, they worshipped both male and female gods, revered many of the feminine principles, and allowed women to participate in every facet of life. Celtic women were druids, bards, queens and warriors. The queens ruled with their husbands or alone.

The Celts were the fiercest warriors the Romans ever came up against. And Boudicca was the greatest leader they ever conquered. But though Celtic men were great and fierce warriors, they had little patience for long wars. They preferred to fight for a couple of days, take what prisoners and booty they could, and ride home to brag about their prowess in battle. Prisoners became slaves who were easily lost when the next skirmish between tribes arose. There was certainly no love lost between the tribes and therefore few lasting alliances.

The tribes' autonomy worked well until they were faced with Roman legions. A hundred years before Boudicca, Julius Caesar conquered the Celts of Gaul (France), but the fierce tribes of southern Britain drove him from their shores. It wasn't until almost a hundred years later, in 43 CE, that the Romans were able to gain a solid foothold. Not wishing to spend too much time or energy on the invading Romans, mostly because it would have taken uniting with their fellow Celts and fighting for long periods of time, most of the tribes gave in to what seemed to be harmless demands—a few taxes and the right to build forts to house troops.

But what seemed harmless in 43 CE became intolerable by 63 CE. The Romans mowed down the great forests in order to build, not merely forts, but cities, and the taxes they demanded were driving the Celts into starvation. The only part of Celtic society the Romans feared were the druid priests, whose magic they believed, prevented them from conquering the entire land of the Britons. To counteract the druids and their magic, Roman soldiers began slaughtering the priests during nighttime raids on the holy oak groves where they held their sacred rites and ceremonies.

In the midst of this horrific period, Queen Boudicca's husband died. In the hopes of preserving at least something for his family and clan, he left one half of the tribal lands to Boudicca, their two teenage daughters, and his people, and the other half to the Romans. But this was not enough for the ruthless Roman governor, who rebuked the generous offer and demanded everything. Boudicca, a formidable warrior and powerful queen, refused. To teach a lesson to the other tribes, the Romans raped Boudicca's teenage daughters, beat her, and left them all to die of their wounds.

But Boudicca was a warrior queen. The brutal beating and humiliation of her daughters drove her to do the impossible. She united the tribes, and with an army numbering more than one-hundred thousand, she marched on the Romans. Her daughters rode beside her in her chariot, fighting at her side, while Boudicca conquered and burned to the ground the three main Roman cities, including London, wiped out several Roman legions, and marched to face the powerful governor, General Suetonius Paulinus, on a battlefield north of London. This was to be the final battle. There were only two legions left, and with her superior numbers, victory was certain. Boudicca was a great woman leader. Unlike her male counterparts, she was able to unite her people and lead them, initially because her cause was just. Unlike male tribal leaders, she fought not for power, but for the most feminine of causes: home, family, and freedom. The Roman historian Tacitus tells us in *The Annals of Imperial Rome*:

"Boudicca drove round all the tribes in a chariot with her daughters in front of her.

'We British are used to woman commanders in war,' she cried. 'I am descended from mighty men! But I am not fighting for my kingdom and wealth now. I am fighting as an ordinary person for my lost freedom, my bruised body, and my outraged daughters.'"

Before that final battle, Boudicca became disheartened by the mood of her warriors. They were so intoxicated with power that they had forgotten the great cause for which they fought, and they had become besotted with drink, women, and booty. Boudicca was so disgusted with them, she was ready to walk away, until she learned that the Romans had slaughtered two thousand druid priests and priestesses who had gathered on the Holy Isle of Anglesey to pray for victory. This was more than Boudicca could stand. She rallied her troops and went once more into battle. But it was useless. Although her troops outnumbered the Romans ten to one, they had fought far past their endurance levels. Men who were used to fighting for two or three days had been fighting for months. Now, after weeks of looting, feasting, drinking, and fornicating, they had lost whatever discipline Boudicca had originally instilled in them. They had been winning repeatedly—what, they thought, could stop them now?

The ground was soggy from three days of torrential rains as Boudicca led her troops onto the battlefield to meet face to face for the first time with the Roman general and governor, Suetonius. The Romans had their backs to the forest, an arrangement that pleased Boudicca, for it would give her the upper hand. The Romans were at a loss in the dense forests of Britain. As was the custom, the families of the Celtic troops arrived to watch the final victory. They pulled their heavy wooden wagons into position at the back of the battlefield and settled in to enjoy the proceedings.

Boudicca and her hordes took the first half of the day. By afternoon, however, her troops were flagging, and Suetonius began to push them back. By the time Boudicca realized that she had not prepared for retreat, it was too late. The Romans drove the Celts back into their own cheering section. Boudicca ordered the wagons out of the way, but the soggy ground made any quick movement impossible. Instead of watching the triumph, the families on their heavy wagons watched in vain as the Celtic warriors fell by the thousands. Boudicca, tortured by her feelings of revulsion and grief for her armies, and outraged by the treachery of the Romans, chose suicide over capture.

Some versions of the story tell that her daughters lived and kept fighting from the north, lands that never surrendered to the Romans.

Though the Romans considered her the empire's most formidable opponent, Boudicca didn't fight—as men often do—for glory. She was driven to it. She did not fight, as Tacitus tells us, for her kingdom and wealth, but for her daughters, her home, and her own bruised body, all feminine values that had been attacked by Imperial Rome, the ancient world's greatest patriarchy. Her bruised body stands as a metaphor for the ravaged land of Britain.

Boudicca's story is historical fact, yet it has many mythic qualities. An outraged mother fights for her daughters. They ride before her in her chariot wielding swords to drive out the destroyer. They are immensely powerful, but they are not successful. They lose. The story echoes hundreds of myths. The Great Mother fighting for her brood. Feminine power sacrificed to the march of patriarchal progress. The great queen killing herself out of despair for her slaughtered people. Feminine values and leadership wiped out by a disciplined masculine force that will bury female leadership for another two thousand years.

And so it did. For two thousand years, men have been taking the leadership role exclusively. They have perfected the act of war to such a point that they are now capable of completely obliterating the human race and much of the animal and plant kingdoms. While Boudicca felt that she was fighting for the feminine principles of family and home, she nevertheless led her armies like a man. She could not win in that situation, because she was going against the true feminine principles of nurture, which is the reverence and preservation of life.

In the late twentieth century, women have fought for equality in all things and were allowed once again into the masculine world of war. Perhaps the most horrifying images from the 2003-2004 War in Iraq are the photographs of the young woman soldier in Baghdad's Abu Ghraib prison posing with thumbs up while leaning over the bloody, tortured bodies of naked Iraqi prisoners. This is not the feminine way of leadership. This is part of the cycle of violence that Power Women leaders are being called upon to end. Like Boudicca, we have a great cause: to fight the patriarchy. But Boudicca used the tools of the patriarchy and lost.

What kind of tools can we use as Authentic Leaders to win?

WE CAN'T GO BACKWARDS

Although there is a great deal we can learn from the prehistoric era, we can never go back. In the Neolithic village, the elders and the shamans led the tribes. They worked in concert with the Mother God and all the Earth Spirits. In those years, humans were directed mostly by impulses from the right side of the brain, which gave them great understanding of the Divine and the Spirit world, but little or no comprehension of the abstract world of thought and symbol. In these societies, the survival of the tribe was paramount. Each person was simply a cog. The well being of the tribe inhabited every thought and drove every decision. The idea of individual freedom, wherein people have unique dreams and desires, had not yet been conceived.

Guiding these ancient peoples were the ancestors. They were prayed to, listened to, revered, and feared. Because permission of the ancestors was required for every major and minor function of the tribe, it was very difficult to make changes, and that made progress slow.

The dominator era developed out of the human race's need to evolve more swiftly, and to do that we had to move into the left side of our brains. This led to abstract thinking, and eventually to the concept of the individual. When we took God out of the Earth and placed "him" in the sky, we separated human beings and God for the first time. This separation created a model for One-Who-is-Above-Others. And with this example to follow, individual men began standing up in front of the tribe and declaring themselves leaders—the one who is above the others.

Moving away from the Mother God and the rules of the ancestors cut us off from many powerful nurturing traditions. It also pushed women into the background of history. But at the same time, this break freed humanity from some stultifying traditions and urged us forward. As leaders emerged and gained power over their tribes, villages, and cities, others began to wish for similar individual notoriety Wars were fought and kingdoms toppled as more people developed a taste for individual power. Ironically, alongside destruction was a brand new idea – that all people are individuals and can have individual rights.

By 600 BCE, the Greeks had invented democracy, a form of government that recognized individuals. But it took another two thousand years for the framers of the United States Constitution to declare that "All men are created equal...they are endowed by their Creator with certain unalienable rights, that among these are life, liberty and the pursuit of happiness." This series of freedoms was inconceivable five thousand years ago, as our ancestors took the first baby steps away from tribal unity. Liberty was unheard of, because to be liberated means to be free of tribal traditions. The pursuit of one's own wants and desires overrides the necessities of the tribe.

At the beginning of the new millennium, we as women find ourselves embracing and celebrating our individual freedom while simultaneously yearning for the nurture of a tribe. A new kind of leader is going to have to emerge to bring these two worlds together.

To learn more about the right and left sides of the brain and their affect on human history read The Alphabet vs. the Goddess, *by Leonard Shlain.*

LEADERS AND GUIDES

As we become more familiar with both the Yin and the Yang parts of ourselves, we will begin to understand the subtleties of leading. Moving into the new paradigm, we become aware that there are actually two parts to the one unifying act of leadership.

The Yang aspect is the part that we have traditionally considered leadership. In the dominator culture, the Yang leader stands in front of the group and directs the action of the followers. In warfare, the leader rides in front shouting directions and leading the charge. But though it has rarely been acknowledged, Yang leaders cannot succeed unless they are balanced and informed by the subtler Yin energy. The native guide or scout in colonial warfare personifies this Yin aspect most dramatically. He was the one who went out ahead, surveyed the territory, and then returned to share his knowledge and consult with the Yang leader. He then rode next to the leader to guide him. It has always been assumed that the Yang leader accomplished all of his great feats on his own. He alone was responsible for his victory. His men followed him. Without him all would be lost. But that has never actually been the case. The guide in empire-building colonial warfare was always the Other, whether this guide was a Native American guide working alongside the leaders of the cavalry as they conquered the American West, or the East Indian guide who helped the British take India. The contributions of these guides to the campaigns they participated in were equal to their famous leader counterparts, but it is a rare occasion when they are acknowledged. Gunga Din is an elegant example of the exception that proves the rule.

The strong woman behind the great man is another example of the guide/leader, Yin/Yang marriage. Other illustrations of this coupling are the corporate president and his lifelong secretary, the farmer and his wife, the ship's captain and first mate.

Now look at this on a personal level. In the last chapter we explored our own inner balance of Yin and Yang. Now, we can expand that idea in order to find our own leadership qualities within our own natures. We can begin to understand the subtle inner guidance that supports us as we take the steps toward our leadership roles in our communities and in the world.

Traditionally, leaders have followers. In a dominator society that is all that can be tolerated. But in a partnership society, followers become superfluous. They will actually hinder progress. A successful partnership society must be peopled with involved participants. As the guide aspect of leadership is recognized and honored, both will become equal in their appeal, so that women and men can move back and forth between the roles of leader and guide with equanimity. In a community where all sit at a "round table" as leaders and guides, there are no followers. Every person becomes responsible for the decisions and actions of the whole, some guiding, some leading, all participating fully, no one blindly subservient to another. And there can never be the excuse, "I was just following orders."

Questions to Ponder

- *Do you find yourself guiding or leading in most of your relationships?*
- *Are you a better leader or guide?*
- *If you prefer to lead, why? If you prefer to guide, why?*
- *Do you consider yourself a follower? If yes, how do you think that impacts the way you feel about leaders?*
- *Do you think you'd like to be a leader? If not, why not?*

HOW DARE YOU PRESUME TO LEAD?!

I moved to Hollywood in the late '60s when a young woman from Brooklyn was beginning to be viewed as a formidable movie presence. Her name was Barbra Streisand. During the shooting of *Hello Dolly*, Streisand began using the power that she had gained from her astronomical box-office success to make suggestions on the set.

A close friend of mine, Danny Lockin, played the role of Barnaby in *Hello Dolly*. Every evening after shooting he'd come over to my house and complain about "the horrible bitch." I was young and impressionable, and I figured my friend must be right. Soon, the press began to echo Danny's complaints and the legend of "Barbra Streisand the monster" was born. As the years went by, and I found myself struggling for success in the "boys' club" called Hollywood, I began to understand what she was up against. Over the years, as other women have dared to take leadership positions in the film business, Streisand has found allies. Thirty years later, she is even occasionally honored for her brave stance and powerful work.

But beneath the adoration, and behind the awards, the stain of her daring still lingers. She is still remembered in the minds of many as "the monster," the woman who stood up and said, "I know more about lighting and staging musical numbers and directing actors than any of you." They said "No!" But she insisted: "Yes!"

Questions to Ponder

- *What is a leader?*
- *What makes a good leader?*
- *Are you afraid of taking a leadership position? If yes, what are you most afraid of?*
- *Have you been thwarted when you've taken leadership roles? How does that make you feel?*

TEEN LEADERS

In the 1950s and '60s, and even in some places in the '70s, junior-high and high-school girls were not encouraged to take leadership roles. Class officers were chosen very distinctly along gender lines. Class president and vice president were, with few exceptions, boys, and the offices of secretary and treasurer went to girls.

Girls were, of course, cheerleaders, but this is a seriously flawed use of the word leader. Beautiful girls jumping up and down urging the boys on the field to victory is one of the patriarchy's sweetest coups. The fact that this display of male aggrandizing was the most coveted leadership position a girl could achieve in high school is a powerful statement about the role of women in that era and still today.

Another way to look at the cheerleader is in the role of guide that we defined earlier. The football champion hero/leader coupled with the cheerleader/guide is one of America's treasured fantasy images. But the thought of that pretty girl having any real participation in the team's victory is not considered.

Despite the opposition, many of us found ways to assert ourselves in smaller, less obvious forums such as language clubs, social clubs, church organizations, as well as scouting, and the few sports in which girls were allowed to participate, such as skating, tennis, and swimming.

When I spoke with my friend Michele, fifty-four, a massage therapist and esthetician, about any memories she had of taking a leadership role during high school, her face lit up.

"Yes," she said, "I used to give sermons at my church. I was in a youth program. I talked about Bob Dylan's poetry and stuff like that. I loved it so much. It was great."

I have known Michele for many years, and this was the first time she ever mentioned this treasured memory. The surge of joy she exuded while talking about giving her sermons was infectious. Michele is one of the brightest women I know, but in the twenty-five years we've been friends, she has never overtly expressed her leadership qualities. I asked her why she didn't keep up her inspirational speaking.

"Life happened," she replied. "After college, I had babies and things just got too hard." Then I asked her if she could see herself stepping into a leadership role in this second half of her life. She told me she would like to be a leader in women's beauty, working to show women how to be more beautiful in the second half of life with non-invasive natural products and treatments.

Even if you don't think of yourself as a leader, there may very well have been a time when you did assert those qualities. Even if it was only once that you stood in front of the class to speak on something you felt passionate about. During the '60s, with the Viet Nam War and the civil rights movement, many young women took stances against war and racial intolerance, because both are contrary to feminine, or Yin, principles. In the 1960s and '70s, more young women made their voices heard standing up for themselves in the women's rights movement.

Questions to Ponder

• *What leaders did you admire in your teen years?*
• *Did you find yourself leading or following as a teenager?*
• *Can you remember particular times in your teen years when you took leadership positions?*

FEAR OF AUTHORITY OR FEAR OF LEADING?

The first definition for authority in Webster's New Collegiate Dictionary is, "The right and power to command, enforce laws, exact obedience, determine or judge." The sixth definition is, "The power to influence or persuade resulting from knowledge or experience."

To lead is to have authority. To lead in the new paradigm as Power Women, authority must grow out of our knowledge and experience, as well as harmony and nurture. Many women who have not considered themselves leaders, may find the new definition more appealing and follow their natural abilities to lead in both the leader and guide roles.

To become Power Women we are asked to question the old patterns, face the terror of new paths, grab the reins, ride through the dark night of the challenge, and come out stronger and more powerful on the other side.

Helen, a sixty-four-year-old scientist in one of my circles, never thought she wanted to be a leader. As a research scientist, her academic career had benefited from the women's movement of the '60s and '70s, but she had been focused on her research and never been political. When she joined one of my circles she was ready to retire and not sure what to do next.

For the first couple of weeks, she held back. She wasn't sure what she thought of the meditation and games. I was afraid she would drop out. Then after the "Second Week: The Power of Creativity," she made a 180-degree turn. For the next seven weeks she did all the games and exercises. She gained insight upon insight about herself through the meditation and journaling. She made her collages, wrote poetry for the first time, and was the first to report on her role model. She was an inspiration to the rest of the women in the circle, who were all younger.

And then we came to "The Power of Authentic Leadership." She arrived late to the circle that night. During the entire evening she was withdrawn. At the end of the evening, she announced that she wouldn't be back. She had a sudden invitation to go with an old colleague on a trip to Asia. That sounded exciting, and I asked if it were possible to postpone it for two weeks. But she assured me it wasn't. I asked if she would take the book and keep doing the work, and she just shook her head.

"I'm done. It's been very interesting, but I don't need to do more."

Helen, who had been the inspiration of the circle, was suddenly cold and aloof. The rest of the women in the circle were crestfallen. I had seen this before. The idea of becoming a leader was the one thing in the course that terrified Helen. She had spent the past ten years alone in a science lab. It had been daring of her to take this course. Yet she had done so well. She had become an integral and much loved member of her circle.

I took her aside and asked what had made her decide to leave so close to completion. She tried to keep up the pretense of the trip to Asia, but after a moment she broke down.

"I can't be a leader. It's not in my nature. I could never be good at it. The rest of the course is about success and freedom. How can I do that when I'm afraid to lead? It's too hypocritical."

I asked if she had ever taught a class or led a discussion. She said that yes, as a professor she'd had to do that. I asked if she considered teaching a leadership position. She shook her head, "no." After a moment she smiled shyly. "Well, I guess it is, isn't it?" And did you hate teaching? "Not teaching, but I hated the politics, that's why I moved into doing research in the last ten years. I couldn't stand all the games and positioning to become head of the department."

I told her that I completely understood. That is why this chapter is called "The Power of Authentic Leadership." It is about changing the old model of leadership. It's about being a guide when you want to and a leader when you want to. We talked for an hour over cold cups of decaf. By the time we locked up and walked to our cars, Helen had come up with several ways that she would change the academic system. I applauded her ideas and told her also that though she had some great ideas to change the system, if she was tired of academia, she was free to find somewhere else to put her talents in her Power Woman years, this time on her own terms.

The following week, Helen was back. The rest of the circle was thrilled. She had done her games and exercises, and she reported to the circle that in her meditation and journaling she had found that her fear of leadership came from watching her father when he led the choir at church. He was a tyrant who belittled people while they were singing holy music. The picture of him leading the choir made her cringe. She had held this as her image of leadership all her life.

Now, she could begin to paint a new picture of leadership for herself.

The patriarchal form of leadership can be frightening or distasteful for women to embrace. We are creating a new kind of leadership. Leading and guiding within community means that we lead sometimes and guide at others, while never giving our power to another. As Power Women we are creating a new way for women to be leaders in the world. We are doing this on behalf of our sisters and ourselves now and for the future. Some of the women in your circle will be more comfortable than others with leadership. Those who feel at ease must be patient and supportive of those who feel less so. That is an important component of Authentic Leadership.

You are now close to the completion of your journey out of the underworld and into your true Power Woman self. This is the point on the journey where some women want to turn back. Don't be one of them. Persevere. There are only two more chapters. Two more points of power to embrace: "Enlightened Success" and "Freedom." Don't let old patterns block your way.

Questions to Ponder

- *How do you feel about people in roles of authority?*
- *Who or what do you consider the main authority in your life?*
- *Do you respect your own authority?*

WHY LEAD?

You may have no desire to become a leader at this point in your life. You may very well feel the way I did a few years ago. I was tired. I'd been fighting the good fight for a long time, and it seemed that it must be my turn to rest and let the younger generation take over. Partly it was the exhaustion of peri-menopause and menopause, when the only leading we can do is getting ourselves through the levels of the underworld. But later, as I began to feel stronger, it occurred to me that while the younger generation may have the physical energy and passion for leadership in this rapidly changing world, what they lack—and I have—is life experience.

We older women have spent the past thirty or so years preparing for leadership. We have developed skills that are mandatory in good leaders. Even if we've never left our homes, as mothers and wives we've honed the fundamental skills of leadership—diplomacy, cost control, scheduling, conflict resolution, decision making, motivating others, and crisis management —to name a few.

"Think positive about our future and work like hell."

That was 94-year-old Doris "Granny D" Haddock's campaign slogan in her bid for U.S. Senator from New Hampshire in 2004. (When this book went to press the election had not been held. Here's hoping that she won.)

Granny D is the ultimate Power Woman leader. Born January 24, 1910, Granny D made headlines when she walked 3,200 miles across the United States at the age of 89 in 1999 to demonstrate her concern for campaign finance reform. Though she dropped out of Boston's Emerson College to marry in 1931, she was awarded an honorary degree 69 years later in 2000. She is only five feet tall and suffers from emphysema and arthritis, but she says that both improved during the three-thousand-mile walk. Random House published her first book, Granny D: You're Never To Old to Raise a Little Hell.

In 2003, she launched an effort to register working women to vote, traveling 22,000 miles around the country to more than 100,000 workplaces.

"I do expect to be around for several more elections," she said, when she began that tour, "but you never know. If this is my last wish tour, then my last wish is that America's women, who worked so hard amid great violence for the right to vote, take that now as a sacred duty in 2004." She was still around in the fall of 2004 and running for the Senate. She promised that she would only run for one term, retiring then at 101.

Read Granny D's inspirational speeches online at http://grannyd.com/speeches.htm.

As travelers on life's journey, and as emerging Power Women, we have certain responsibilities. One of these is to pass on the knowledge and information we've gained to the younger generation. They have the passion. We have the experience. Together we can make beautiful music.

In the '60s, there was a saying, "If you're not part of the solution, you're part of the problem." Forty years later this is still true. With our skills, natural sense of fair play, and passion for beauty and nature, women can be brilliant, exciting leaders. We come armed with new ideas, new plans of action, and a new sense of individual and communal harmony. Why not lead?

GAMES AND EXERCISES

WEEK NINE: THE POWER OF AUTHENTIC LEADERSHIP

1. Make a list of 10 qualities you think are important for a leader to have.

2. Make a list of twenty world leaders, men and women, throughout history whom you admire.

3. Go shopping. Try on clothes that make you feel like a leader. You don't have to buy anything, just try them on. And don't get stuck in the idea that you have to wear business suits to be a leader. You're a woman. You love beauty. Try flowing things, long and short things, clothes in all shapes and colors. See what kind of clothing inspires you to leadership, or that supports the most powerful part of your leadership personality. Have a ball!

4. Name five leaders from your adolescent years. How did they make you feel then? How do they make you feel now?

5. Think about the times your role model was challenged in her leadership role. Have a discussion in your circle about your role model's leadership and how she triumphed over the obstacles.

REMEMBER to journal and meditate daily. Write about becoming a leader in your journaling. In your meditations ask your Spirit self to show you what you look like as a leader.

THE POWER OF

Enlightened Success

"I always tell people who are depressed about getting older,
Do what you really want to do and don't let anybody stop you,
And that will make you feel as though the world is really yours.
Do your dream, go for it, do it now! Take a chance, speak up.
What can you lose? Only your regrets."

– Anna Kainen

We are taking the next to the last step before crossing the threshold into our new Power Woman expression. To reach the final step and the Power of Freedom, we must first examine success, what it has meant to us in the past, and what it can be for us in the future. In this chapter we are going to redefine success, so that we can embrace it and let it into our lives.

The word success has an almost magical ring to it. Say it. SUCCESS! Listen to it. SUCCESS! The resonance in the heart is like a reverie. We dream of success. We long for success. We plan for success, and we support our partners, our children, and our friends as they strive for and often achieve success.

But if we haven't yet attained what we consider to be success, we may have become resentful of our partner's, our friends', or even our children's successes. And though we may have become successful in our careers, we may still yearn for success in different contexts, or for different accomplishments. A woman who has a successful law practice can feel like a failure if her original dream of success was to be a wildlife photographer.

The choices we made in our young adult years were often directed by the desires others held for us, by a society that didn't support women's bigger dreams, and by the necessity to focus on our children. I had a successful career as a production accountant in the film industry. My family was very proud of me. But my dream was to write movies, not count their costs. When, at forty-six, I renounced my lucrative accounting career for the uncertainties of a writer's life, many of those near and dear to me were horrified. They talked about how successful I was. They couldn't understand this sudden change. They didn't realize how unsuccessful I felt. Eschewing one's dreams, no matter how good the cause may be, scars the soul. At midlife, at the birthing of our new selves, it is time to become truly successful at what our souls desire.

Questions to Ponder

- *What does success mean to you?*
- *Who in your personal acquaintance did you consider successful in your youth?*
- *What kind of successes have you striven for in your life?*

WHY NOT ME?

The desire to succeed is deeply rooted in all people. Not succeeding is crippling. Many of us can look at our mothers for examples of the effect that not succeeding beyond the home has on older women. As a sex we are quite practiced at suppressing the pain of failing to succeed. We were taught as teenagers to let the boys win, to not be selfish, and to never take the best for ourselves. We were taught that competition was unladylike and that our success lay not in our achievements in the world, but in the bosom of our families. And, of course, those of us who are mothers, did/do need to focus on our children. Raising healthy, happy children is a success that we can and must celebrate. But in the second half of life we are ready to move into new successes.

No one consciously plans to not succeed. No one purposely goes through life making one unsuccessful attempt after another at achieving her dreams. But the obstacles standing in the way of success are often more than we can overcome. We may find ourselves standing on the sidelines watching others achieve success and finally cave in to the false "reality" that there is no way we are ever going to have similar success. We may have grown envious, angry, despairing, and even resigned to the fact that success might never be ours. By the time we have reached our forties and fifties, many of us have given up all hope of finding the success we dreamed of in our teens. Some experts correlate difficult menopause with the lack of successfully achieving our dreams in the years preceding it.

Even if you have achieved some success, you may not have had the awareness to realize and embrace it. In our society there is an ever-upward spiraling expectation cycle that keeps us from taking the breathing time to recognize the successes we have achieved.

If you find yourself standing on the sidelines of your dreamed-of life, applauding others, and secretly asking, "Why not me?" it is time to step into the road and decide to succeed. Using your journaling and your meditation tools you can begin to uncover the psychological and emotional obstacles that block your way to success.

As you reveal the old beliefs that kept you from succeeding, you must first, quickly, overcome the urge to feel sorry for yourself. Practice tough love on yourself. Love yourself enough to see that every minute you spend on self-pity encroaches on the time you have to enjoy your success.

Having exposed old beliefs and blockages, begin to imagine yourself as a successful human being. To be something splendid, we have to be able to imagine it first. We all have great imaginations, though we may not be aware of the fact. Too much emphasis is placed on the practical in our society, and imagination is often relegated to the frivolous. In truth, there can be no success without imagination. No invention was ever created without the inventor imagining it first.

Once you have imagined yourself successful, allow your heart to open and experience what it feels like to be successful. Don't be surprised if tears begin to flow. If this is a feeling you haven't experienced much in your life, it can be a bit overwhelming. Accept it and cry for joy.

FEAR OF SUCCESS AND FEAR OF FAILURE—THE SAME THING?

The word success alone can create an atmosphere of fear. Some of us reel away from the idea of success, while others of us are more terrified of failure. How we react to success or failure is instilled by our parents' expectations. A parent, who has achieved a great deal of success in her or his own life, may expect as much or more from her or his offspring. On the other hand, a parent who sees her or himself as a failure, may have little or no expectations of success for her or his children, and in fact can often-times be jealous of a child's potential for success.

My mother had no experience of personal success. Having been moth-erless from early childhood and brought up in foster homes, she had no one who expected anything from her. Though she was a strong woman, who made a seemingly comfortable life, she didn't feel that she was in any way successful. Life had dealt her a difficult hand—from the loss of her mother to the loss of her first-born—and she was terribly embittered.

She focused most of that bitterness on me. When, in my early teens, I expressed a desire to succeed in a way that was outside my mother's realm of understanding, she was suddenly faced with what she perceived to be her lack of success. Consciously or subconsciously, she became jealous of my potential and the life ahead of me. And like all children who are hyper-sensitive to the atmosphere around them, I was aware that if I succeeded it would make my mother very angry.

I persevered, I persisted, I worked hard to succeed, but found myself just missing success again and again. For me to succeed threatened the most basic need we all have, to be loved by our mothers, and in my adolescent mind, success would have meant losing her love. It took many years before I could overcome that fear.

Claudia, fifty-two, is the daughter of a successful doctor and an alcoholic, socialite mother, who had never found success in her life. Claudia, who is a stunning woman, was an extremely pretty only child. The one thing that marred her beauty was her terrible anger, which, she told me, she took out on other girls by stealing their boyfriends.

When she was in high school, she dreamed of becoming a doctor like her father, whom she adored. The last thing Claudia's mother wanted was for her daughter to achieve success, especially in her husband's world of medicine, from which she felt excluded. She was profoundly jealous of Claudia's beauty and of her father's love.

She belittled Claudia daily, telling her how foolish it was for a girl with such a low IQ to hope to get into med school. By the time Claudia went to college, she had given up all hope of becoming a doctor. She got her nursing degree, and instead of being a doctor, she married one.

Two years ago, her husband asked for a divorce and since then, Claudia has been able to spend time on herself. She has begun to realize how intelligent she really is and that she could have made it through med school with ease. She recently applied and was accepted into UCLA medical school, yet she still harbors a fear of succeeding. Her mother, dead from alcoholism for five years, still haunts her. Claudia's success is partly measured in how she is persisting in spite of her fears.

If we are not afraid of success, we may find that we are afraid of failure. Some families base everything on economic and/or professional success. You live or die by how much success you achieve. To fail is to lose your parents' love and respect. The daughters of these families can be extremely successful in their careers or in marrying well, because they are driven by their fear of failure to live up to their parents' expectations.

Others in the same family can be driven to mutiny, choosing failure as their means to achieve rebellion. The success in these kind of families is measured by the families' idea of what success is, which only rarely coincides with their daughters' dreams and desires.

In more balanced families, a daughter might simply fear disappointing her parents if she weren't to succeed. And this fear can make her work harder to achieve success in order to enjoy it with her proud and happy parents.

But whether we are driven by fear of success or fear of failure, we are still ensconced in fear, and fear, though it can be a motivator for success, is still a negative energy that keeps us off-balance and out of the natural flow of our life's purpose. True success is success born from love by following our soul's direction.

Questions to Ponder

- *Have you ever felt like you might be afraid of success?*
- *Have you ever felt the fear of failure?*
- *Do you have any bad feelings around the idea of success or failure? If you do, define them as best you can.*
- *Have you ever been on the verge of success and then pulled back from it? If so, how often can you remember doing it?*

INANNA'S SUCCESS

While Inanna hung on the meat hook, murdered by her own sister, she was at the very heart of darkness. There was no way out. She could do nothing to save herself. All hope of a successful return to Earth was forfeited. But at the same time back on Earth and in the heavens, other forces were working to promote her successful return.

Inanna's assistant prevailed upon the Gods of Heaven to save Inanna. Though two gods refused, the transgendered god Enki agreed to help. Enki created two little creatures, described as sexless devotees. These little creatures, presumably because they were sexless, could descend undetected into the center of the netherworld. There they found Inanna, and the magic that they carried from Heaven empowered the goddess to rise from death and make her ascent back through the seven gates of hell and onto the Earth. Her successful return to Earth and Heaven is one of the most powerful feminine images in all literature. She returns not as a loving, acquiescent wife and mother, but as the fierce champion of the whole world.

Although Inanna set her rescue and ultimate triumphant return in motion before she entered hell—having charged her servant Ninshubur to go for help if she failed to return—once she was in the Underworld, she had no power over the outcome of her adventure. Her success was left in the hands of the gods.

As we seek success in the second half of our lives, we must, like Inanna, have the faith to launch ourselves headlong into our purpose. We must prepare, as much as possible, but once we're on our way, we cannot cling to expectations or hoped-for outcomes. Success will come if we simply succumb to our purpose and do our work.

DREAMS OF TEENS

As teenage girls, we all had dreams of success. Few of us had support for those dreams. But, girl, did we dream! Tragically, many did not believe in their ability to succeed. As I've taught this course and counseled hundreds of women, who were teenagers in the 1950s, '60s, and even into the '70s, I've discovered that the vast majority had no hope of achieving success in anything outside of marriage and motherhood.

Jeannine, a fifty-three-year-old tax accountant, told me that in her first year of high school she was invited to join a sorority.

"There was an elaborate initiation process. I had passed all kinds of tests to assure the group that I was the kind of girl they would want to have as a member of their private society. On the final evening, I was asked to stand up in front of everyone and answer a short list of questions. They said that as soon I answered some simple questions I would be voted into the sorority. Everyone was sure that I would make it in with flying colors.

"I stood in front of the fireplace in the living room of a very ordinary middle-class house in the suburbs of Cleveland. I remember very clearly that I was wearing black-and-white plaid Bermuda shorts with a white button-down collar blouse and a red crewneck sweater. I was tall – five-foot eight – and when I stood up, I towered over all the very small girls seated on the floor around me. Suddenly, I felt horribly uncomfortable, but I reminded myself that these were simple questions, and it would all be over shortly.

"One of the senior members asked me the first question, which was, 'Where did I live and how long had I lived there?'

"I'd lived in the same house since I was born, so that was a breeze. Then one of the officers asked me for my parents' first names. I was beginning to relax a little. The next question from a girl in the back, whom I didn't recognize, was what my father did for a living. I said he was a public accountant." Jeanine smiled at this.

"I was feeling pretty good by this time. Then someone announced that the next question would be the final one. I could feel tension in the room. I knew that I was a hair's breadth away from being welcomed into a very prestigious club. The president asked me the final question. She was one of those girls whose hair was always perfect.

"'How much money does your father make a year?'

"I was really shocked. My parents taught me that it was very bad etiquette to ask anyone how much money they made, and that it was equally bad form to tell anyone how much money you had."

Jeanine didn't know what to say. *"Everyone was waiting for me. I saw my friend, who had sponsored me, nodding at me to go ahead. I had to say something, so I lied. I looked straight at them and said that I didn't know how much money my father made. I said that it wasn't ever discussed in my family. That wasn't much of a lie really. My mother had told me once, but we never really discussed it."*

Jeanine stared down at a sea of unbelieving faces. The president told her that she could call her parents and get the information, or she would be asked to leave. *"I knew that if I called my mother and asked her, she'd tell me that it wasn't their business, so I asked if I could go home and talk to my parents and come back on another day. The officers huddled briefly*

and then came back with their decision. No! I could call now,
or my membership application would be terminated immediately.
I felt the heat rising in my face as I turned to find my purse.
My friend was looking at me with horror, as though I'd just
committed murder."

Walking home alone, Jeanine wondered why she'd been so
stubborn. After all, her parents would probably never have found
out. But there was something about being judged by her father's
monetary success that rubbed her the wrong way.

"I consider this incident one of my first successes," she
told me.

Early successes were often based on who or what our family was or had. If we came from a wealthy family, or had parents who were respected in the community, we may have received honors simply because of our connection. Those of us from less well-off families may have found that success came less easily. But we all had dreams of success that reached far beyond the petty boundaries of our parents' status or financial worth, and when we achieved things for ourselves they were all the sweeter. Some of us dreamed of being successful scientists, musicians, writers, or artists. These dreams were often stifled by our families' staunch beliefs in what women "should" do with their lives. A young lady from a "good family" was expected to do certain things, the most important of which was to marry "well." That is, marry a boy in her social class, race, and religion, with good prospects, while a girl from a blue-collar family was expected to marry a nice boy from the neighborhood, and get a job to help out until the children came. Still others were quelled by circumstance. Girls who had big plans for their future success despite the wishes of parents could find themselves pregnant and married before they got up the nerve to leave town. After ten years and three or four babies, the dreams for success lacked their initial luster and were remembered only as girlhood foolishness.

Sandy, forty-nine, a frustrated painter and the mother of three, has been raising her two younger children alone for the past ten years. Her oldest daughter is grown, her second daughter just started college, and her son is in his last year of high school.

When Sandy was in high school, she won a statewide award for her painting. On the day she accepted her prize, she made a plan to go to Paris as soon as she graduated and determined to spend her life painting. In Paris, the aura of great art and artists of an earlier age would inspire her talent. Sandy's parents sent her to a small, private college, and promised that she could go to Paris after she graduated.

Paris was put off forever when Sandy got pregnant during her senior year and married her college sweetheart. She adores her children and said she would never trade them for a life as a painter in Paris. I urged her to return to painting, but she said she didn't think she had the energy.

"Life takes too much out of you. Anyway, it wouldn't be the same going to live in Europe in my fifties," she told me. The sadness in her eyes made me want to cry. In her sewing room, she showed me some paintings she did a few years ago. They were stored behind a pile of boxes. She is very talented. I have a hunch that after her last child leaves for college and she completes her menopause, she'll feel more energetic and ready to go for her dream.

Dreams don't die; they just bury themselves under the junk in the back of the closet, waiting to be liberated.

As teens, our ideas of success were more about fulfilling our dreams than about achieving money or social status. Don't get me wrong. I don't believe that as teenagers we were great humanitarians. We also dreamed of beautiful clothes, handsome guys, and glamorous lives. But when you travel back in time and get to know your teenage self, you find that deep in her heart the dream of success is anchored in a sincere desire for what will bring her, not wealth and status, but joy and fulfillment.

Questions to Ponder

- *Did your parents encourage your success when you were young?*
- *Have your parents or partners ever discouraged your striving for success? If yes, can you remember how you felt when they did?*

SUCCESS WITHOUT THE STRESS

Achieving what we have come to define as success in our current culture is extremely stressful. The majority of people who succeed must strive hard to overcome obstacles. They must work countless hours while others who are less driven rest or sleep. They must be competitive and ready to put their success above everything else in their lives.

For a lot of women, this was, and is, too high a price to pay. Even with careers that they love, most women cannot compete for success with the same drive as men, because quality of life and the value of family and friends are more important to them.

For the past decade, there's been a lot of talk about the "Supermom," the woman who has it all—career, family, friends, success, and, above all, STRESS. There doesn't seem to be any way around the stress. By the time menopause hits, all we who have striven hard want to do is collapse. For those who still have kids at home, this is impossible. Those of us without children, or whose children are grown, have a little more leeway.

Menopause is a time when we should relax. We should create a womb and crawl into it while we gestate. In a perfect world, we would all be able to do that. But the human race hasn't reached that level of enlightenment yet, so we have to get creative. We have to find ways to incorporate our healing and birthing time into our regular lives. We created a room of our own. We've learned to meditate to ease stress and to release tension. We have begun to journal every day to get things off our chest. And we have begun to honor ourselves.

Using these tools and techniques, we can move through menopause and come out on the other side energized and eager for the next step. The two things I hear women expressing a desire for over and over again are less stress and more success.

Nothing we achieve is stress-free, but by adding meditation to our daily lives we can reduce the tension immensely. Twenty minutes of meditation, and twenty minutes of journaling each day will lengthen our days, teach us to prioritize, and help us breath more easily as we move through the day. Meditation is our connection to the Divine. When we are linked up to the universal life force, we suddenly aren't alone. We don't have to handle everything ourselves. How many controlling women do you know? In my crowd, I would say at least ninety percent are what we call "control freaks." This absurd notion that it is our responsibility, alone, to handle everything in our lives and in the lives of our families, keeps our blood pressure up and our stress level at a fevered pitch. But by connecting through meditation to a greater force, we are finally able to let go and allow the universe to carry the major load. With this kind of help, we can expect success to be ours in the second half of life.

LIFETIME MANAGEMENT

In the past, women lived much shorter lives. Life after menopause, as we've learned in earlier chapters, was brief. But this has changed. In the new millennium we will live healthy lives for forty to fifty years after menopause. What if we had known that when we began our adult lives? What impact might it have had on our decisions? What if we knew when we were twenty that we could have babies and raise a family in the first half of our adult lives and then move into meaningful careers in the second half? Some of us may have chosen career over family anyway. But for others that alternative may have given them the freedom to have it all—in stages.

As we step into our power in the second half of life, opening to our purpose, creating new careers, and becoming successful Power Women, we will be setting strong examples for women in the generations to follow. I see a future when young women spend a few years working in their chosen fields, then eagerly become stay-at-home moms in their late twenties, knowing they will have the chance to become Power Women after their children are grown and they've completed their menopause.

I see men slowing down as they come to midlife, as they prepare to move into the home and become supportive partners of their focused, out-of-the-home Power Women wives.

With similar visions for the future in mind, let us prepare the way for the mid-life women who will come behind us by embracing our own power in the second half of life. By embracing the idea that now is the time for us to step out into the world and achieve enlightened success.

Questions to Ponder

- *Do you think a woman's definition of success might be different from a man's? If so, how might it be different?*
- *Do you remember ever being mentored for success? If so how did that feel?*
- *Did anyone ever laugh at you or deride you for desiring success? If yes, how did that feel? What did you do with those feelings?*
- *Who or what has kept you from achieving success? Do you harbor resentment toward these people or events? How do you think you can diffuse it?*

NEW STANDARDS OF SUCCESS

The old ways of achieving or experiencing success no longer serve the planet or the way women like to live on it. The competitive dog-eat-dog world one must enter to achieve success repels me. As I look back over my twenty years working in the film industry in Hollywood, I realize that that model of success contributed to my failure to achieve what I longed for. I wasn't able to adjust my emotional senses to a setting that would numb me enough to play in that arena.

In the '80s, a popular bumpersticker declared: "He who dies with the most toys wins." For most of the 1980s and '90s a lot of people believed that conspicuous consumption signified success and having more of something than somebody else basically defines success in dominator cultures. Competition plays a major role in how we measure success, the prizes being political power, priestly power, intellectual snobbery, social status, or just having more sons than the man next door.

This false sense of success insinuates itself insidiously into our daily lives. For example, you may have had a wonderful year and are feeling very proud of yourself and the success you've achieved, when someone in your crowd gets a new car. At first, you may feel a little jealous, but you're happy for them. Then another friend buys a new car. Suddenly, all of the pride in your success evaporates, and you find yourself needing to buy a new car so that you will feel successful again. It is addictive, a vicious cycle.

There was a time in the '60s and early '70s, when people of the counterculture shunned money as a measure of success. A person's commitment to social activism was the highest measure of success. A large percentage of that very same counterculture gave up those values in exchange for "the most toys wins" philosophy in the '80s and '90s, but many are returning to their roots as they reach midlife and begin remembering where their truth lies.

Real success means moving into harmony with our life's purpose. Our Spirit is constantly pushing us toward our purpose and insisting that we listen more fully so as not to misinterpret this soul-urge. Ambition pushes us toward the dominator model of success. Our soul's yearning nudges us toward our heart's true desire.

Each one of us must create our own definition of success. Once we've defined it, we can begin to move toward achieving it, one step at a time. We can leave the stress and competition behind and begin moving toward our purpose with the guidance and support from our Spirit. In this mode, success can be measured by the joy derived from each new revelation of your purpose, no matter how large or how small. It is in the subtleties that the greatest strides are made. Success comes as we allow the whispered direction of our Spirit to guide us.

Stress-less success is absolutely possible. It takes surrendering to a higher power. It takes tuning in, focusing your awareness, and being as conscious as possible moment by moment. Revel in your accomplishments. Celebrate each day. See success in the small victories over adversity. Eschew the old belief systems, which keep you attached to outcomes. Practice each day at disconnecting from old definitions of success, which hold you back from your real success as a woman in midlife preparing to step into your true power.

As we make these changes in ourselves, we are changing the world around us. As we help create a more loving and supportive world, we are creating a place to live that will be supportive of our hearts' desires. It is a perfect circle. Embrace it and embrace yourself.

SISTERHOOD AND SUCCESS

The most enjoyable way to work and achieve success is with like-minded others. A group of women who are consciously working toward their own individual purpose and success can make powerful differences. Remember that you are not alone. We are all part of great family known as the human race. Remember you have a responsibility to achieve your purpose as part of our human family and as a member of the planet Earth. This is why we sit in circle, to remember and rekindle the fires of our interdependence. We are moving from an era when the individual was a separate entity into an era where the individual will maintain her unique-ness as a member of a team. Become a team player who can both lead and guide when appropriate. This is where your enlightened success lies.

GAMES AND EXERCISES

WEEK TEN: THE POWER OF ENLIGHTENED SUCCESS

1. Find another picture of yourself from when you were sixteen or seventeen years old. Put her on your dresser or on your refrigerator door. Every morning and every night ask the girl in the photo what she really wants to succeed at. (If you have no photos of yourself, find a picture from a magazine that reminds you of yourself as a teenager.)

2. Begin reading through all your morning journals. You can do this over the next period of time before the final ceremony. Jot down notes about anything that appears to be a theme on which you may still want to focus your healing attention or any insights that seem important.

3. List of Successes

    a. Make a list of ten successes you have had throughout your entire life. They may be big or small.

    b. Read over the list. As you read, become aware of how you feel in your heart about each one of these successes. Linger over each success. Remember as much as possible the way you felt when you achieved this success.

    c. Make some kind of notation next to each success that succinctly expresses your feelings around this success. Make up your own system. For instance: Cool, Sweet, Okay, Powerful, Joyous, Rocked My World, Ho Hum, Wow!

    d. Go over the list again and ask yourself which successes make you feel the happiest? Choose the top three successes on your list.

e. Close your eyes, go up to your Sacred Room, light your Star, and expand it ten feet in diameter, until you're completely surrounded by white light. Once you're sitting in the ten-foot White Star, think of your three top successes. As you do, let yourself experience any negative feelings that may be attached to these successes, and drop them into the light and let the light consume them.

Begin now to look for the positive feelings that you have around these happiest of successes. Let these positive feelings expand and grow. If more negative thoughts and feelings come up, such as feelings of guilt for being successful, memories of jealous friends or family, feelings of misplaced remorse, acknowledge them briefly and send them into the light. Focus your awareness on happiness and joy. Sit for a few moments and let this exercise sink deep into your heart.

4. Look through your music collection. Pull out at least three CDs or tapes that make you feel like dancing. Wait until you have the house to yourself. Put on the music. Blast it! Take off your shoes and dance for at least 20 minutes. Please feel free to do this exercise as many times and for as long as you want.

REMEMBER to journal and meditate daily. Focus part of your journaling on how you can find stress-less success. During your meditations in your Sacred Room, ask your Spirit self to become your partner in stress-less success.

THE POWER OF

Freedom

"I saw a woman sleeping.
In her sleep she dreamt life
stood before her, and held in each
hand a gift—in one hand love, in the
other freedom. And she said to the
woman, 'Choose.' And the woman
waited long: and she said, 'Freedom.'
And life said, 'Thou hast well
chosen. If thou hadst said "love"
I would have given thee that
thou didst ask for, I would
have gone from thee, and
returned to thee no more.
Now, that day will come
when I shall return.
In that day I shall bear
both gifts in one hand.'"

– Olive Schreiner

The final step on the journey to embracing our Power Woman is the Power of Freedom. Freedom, like everything else of value on Earth, is acquired in degrees. When we receive a gift without being prepared for it, we often don't recognize its worth and end up squandering it or simply ignoring it.

Women in western society have gained an enormous amount of freedom over the last one hundred years. We've gained the right to vote, to go to college, to hold jobs that traditionally belonged to men. We have sexual freedom. We have become leaders in business, industry, the arts, politics, and more. And yet many of us still feel tethered by old rules and traditions, unable to break out and soar to the heights to which we aspire. Fear and complacency are the only things now holding us back.

As we explore the Power of Freedom we will face those fears and the inertia—the progenitor of complacency—in order to let them go. Once we can fully embrace our inner freedom, our Power Woman will be ready to take on whatever comes her way.

The Power of Freedom is the final Point of Power, because it takes a strong woman to claim her freedom. Freedom is offered to us by life, but many women turn their backs on it, choosing less challenging paths. Through the course of this work, you have constructed a powerful framework on which to build your freedom. It is time to claim it.

 ## THE LONG ROAD TOWARD FREEDOM

"When anything gets freed, a zest goes around the world."

– Hortense Calisher

Humanity has been in pursuit of individual freedom since we left the comfort of Neolithic tribal life. During the Neolithic era, with the domestication of animals and cultivation of crops, the roaming tribes settled into relative comfort—the cold winters could be spent indoors in front of fires, with food harvested in the fall and stored for winter use. Women, who once foraged even in the coldest of seasons, now spent the winters spinning, weaving, and sewing, while the men, who had hunted all winter long, were afforded time to carve wooden utensils, tools, and furniture, and sew hides, tanned in the summer, into shoes and clothes and carrying bags. This early freedom from the constant search for food was a great luxury, and we thrived for several thousand years in this way. No thought was given yet to individual freedom.

Then around five thousand years ago, we began to seek individuation from tribal conformity. Individuals stepped up and demanded to be acknowledged as tribal leaders, set apart by being set above. These leaders, mainly men, were seeking freedom from the tribal laws for themselves, while the rest of the people remained conforming members of the tribe. Two thousand years later, in civilizations such as Greece, Rome, and India, larger groups of men began to demand political freedom. This resulted in male members of the upper classes being designated as citizens and given the opportunity to participate in the governing process.

Thus, freedom was expanded beyond the rulers and a new group of individuals enjoyed political freedom and were called citizens. This movement in Greece is considered the birth of democracy, but since these free citizens kept slaves, and women were no freer and often less free than the slaves they commanded, there was a long way to go toward true democracy.

With the fall of Rome, the idea of a citizen class and greater individual freedom went into abeyance for a thousand years, while the ruling class held sway. Though actual slavery disappeared in Europe during the Middle Ages, serfs who worked the land for the medieval nobility had no rights. Finally in the Renaissance, the idea of individual freedom resurfaced. During this era, while the European ruling class turned their focus of domination from the home front to the broader world—with an eye to creating empires around the globe based on colonial, slave economies—the desire for individual freedom was growing among the common people.

Even as royal fleets and armies conquered and enslaved millions, individuals fought for freedom in Europe, first for religious freedom sparked in the early sixteenth century by Martin Luther's break with the Roman Catholic Church. As religious freedom was gained, the people began to seek political freedom. The United States of America was founded on the beliefs in those two freedoms. The American Revolution—which nevertheless continued to deny equal rights to Africans and women— sparked the French Revolution, and the rest of Europe followed. Finally in the middle of the nineteenth century, slavery was abolished in the United States. Today, many nations throughout the world enjoy a certain amount of political and religious freedom, but there is a long way to go before we can consider this a free world.

In the mid-nineteenth century, women joined the fray to demand the rights of their male counterparts. Even today, at the beginning of the twenty-first century, the largest population of enslaved people on Earth is women. In most developing countries, women continue to live without any freedoms. Even where women are allowed to participate in the political process, we still carry the bonds of a slavery that is seated, not in the constitution, but in the hearts and minds of the dominator society.

Women have always craved freedom as much or perhaps more than men do. But few women adhere to the tenet of violence as a way to achieve that freedom. We have stood behind our revolutionary-minded men in the past, supporting their efforts while abhorring their tactics. Now, as we strive to achieve our own freedom, we do not choose their methods. The political freedoms that we have attained over the past one hundred and fifty years were all won with perseverance and tenacity, not with guns and bombs.

Questions to Ponder

- *What does freedom mean to you?*
- *Do you feel free? If yes, in what ways? If no, in what ways?*
- *Who do you know who exemplifies a free person?*

LYSISTRATA

Women were never emancipated in ancient Greece, yet one powerful woman demanded a freedom that is completely feminine, the freedom from war. The Greek dramatist Aristophanes, who lampooned war and its demagogues in his comedies, brought the story of Lysistrata to the stage in 415 BCE, during the twenty-first year of the twenty-five-year-long Peloponnesian War between the city-states of Athens and Sparta.

Lysistrata, the fictional wife of an Athenian leader, is exhausted by the life that war imposes on women and decides to do something about it. After much consideration, she lights on an idea to end the fighting. She calls all the women of the warring cities to a meeting to reveal her plan. When everyone is gathered, and all the women have pledged their hatred for war, Lysistrata reveals her plan. It is simple: all they have to do is deny their husbands access to their beds until they stop the war. The women aren't anxious to give up the joys of sex, but Lysistrata insists that it will be for only a short time. Men, she explains, will not go without sex for long. Soon they will make peace, and rush back to their women's beds.

Recognizing the truth in Lysistrata's argument, the women from both warring cities agree to the plan. The only fear is that the city's treasury, stored in the Acropolis, will be used by the politicians to bring in outside, mercenary armies.

"Ah! But we have seen to that too," Lysistrata says. "This very day, the Acropolis will be in our hands. That is the task assigned to the older women; while we are here in council, they are going, under pretence of offering sacrifice, to seize the citadel and hold the treasury."

The younger women go home to do their part and rebuke their husbands, while the older women take their stand in the Acropolis. The men plead for entrance to their homes and beds, but the women remain steadfast. Without access to the treasury, and therefore without funds, the exhausted and sexually frustrated men finally come humbly to Lysistrata, who stands before them and delivers the terms—give up war and regain your sexual privileges. In Aristophanes' comedy, the women win, the war ends, and all live peacefully.

Unfortunately, this is a fiction and not history. But Lysistrata gives us a wonderful example of how women united can win without violence. Without sex and money, the men have no power to continue their destructive behavior. The story, written to entertain, was intended as a sex comedy, and so it is the withholding of sex that we remember when we think of the triumph of Lysistrata. But sex is only one part of the plan. Lysistrata knows that the money must also be withheld. The soldiers without sex and the politicians without money will not be able to maintain a war. The younger women deny the sexual needs of the men, while the older women deny them their monetary needs, and the plan works to perfection.

As we consider our own freedom, we must keep in mind that millions of our sisters worldwide are not free. When we look at laws throughout the world that forbid reproductive freedom and family planning, and see that even in our own country a patriarchal structure still opposes women's freedom of choice, we must remember that as the older women we must make a stand, take the citadel, and hold it for the younger women. Each woman's freedom is our own freedom.

Questions to Ponder

- *Can you think of examples in history or in literature in which women worked for freedom and won?*
- *What kinds of freedoms do you think are needed in the world?*
- *What kinds of freedoms are you willing to work for?*

BORN FREE

As teenagers, many of us were confused and frustrated by what was touted as a free country because we found so little freedom for ourselves. We heard that we were all free to grow up to be president. But they weren't talking about us. "All men are created equal." There was no mention in the history books about women being created equal. We were free to be anything we chose in this great land of ours, they said. But that wasn't true at all. We were free to be anything our parents and our society deemed we should be. Freedom wasn't ours. It was our brothers'…maybe. My parents said I was free to do anything I wanted to do. But when I became a political activist, they locked me in my room and forbade me to march for civil rights. I was free to be what seemed fitting for a young lady of my circumstance to be, nothing more. I crawled out the bathroom window and went to the civil rights march. Three days later, I turned eighteen and I left my parents' home forever.

Lisa and Margie, both in their mid-fifties, have been best friends since high school. When they were in their first year of college in 1966, Lisa was raped by her priest and became pregnant. She told no one except Margie and even that was extremely difficult for her. Like so many women in that era, Lisa believed that she must have done something to encourage the rape. She had no idea what to do. She couldn't go to her mother, who would never believe that a priest would do such a thing. She couldn't ask the priest to marry her. And she couldn't have the baby, because everyone would want to know who the father was, and she was sure, even if she told, that no one would believe her. Margie suggested that she get an abortion, but this was seven years before the Supreme Court legalized abortions with Roe vs. Wade, and a year before California legalized abortions of pregnancies caused by rape or incest. The only way to get an abortion in 1966 was in a back-room abortion in the United States or in Mexico.

The two young women did some research and found an actual medical doctor in Tijuana, Mexico, who would perform the operation. They put their money together, still came up short, and borrowed two hundred more to pay the $400 fee. They left their home in Fresno, California, and headed for Mexico. They arrived in Tijuana just after dark.

Following instructions received from their underground source, they made a phone call as soon as they crossed the border. The person on the phone directed them to a bar in the main part of Tijuana. There they waited by a pay phone until they received a call directing them to follow a black car parked two blocks away.

They were terrified. They "tailed" the black car through alleys and back streets and finally out of town to a tiny cinderblock house while pretending to be spies in a James Bond film.

"The black car stopped in front of one of the houses," Lisa recalls, "and the driver pointed to the door. Then he just drove away and left us there."

"We were both trembling getting out of the car," Margie remembers. "And when the door opened, there were these two Dobermans straining at a leash barking at us. It was very, very scary."

The dogs held the girls at bay until they identified themselves to the satisfaction of a man inside. "Once we got inside, we followed the man into a small dressing room. Lisa put on a hospital gown, and then we just sat there waiting for what seemed like an eternity."

At last the doctor arrived. He was a young man, who seemed quite professional under the circumstances, which made them feel a little less frightened. He told Lisa that he had a medical degree in Mexico, and that he did abortions because he believed in them politically. Margie said she was ready to drag Lisa out the place if she felt it was necessary, but the doctor relieved her fears, and Lisa was satistified.

The two young women made the decision together to go ahead with the abortion. Margie was allowed to stay, and she held Lisa's hand as she went under the anesthesia.

"I fainted halfway through the procedure, and Lisa woke me up after it was all over. I was humiliated by my lack of stamina, but everything turned out okay anyway."

Two hours after their arrival, they got back into Margie's car. From out of nowhere the black car appeared, and they followed it back to the border.

A trained doctor treated Lisa in a clean clinic. But many stories did not end up this way. There are a million stories of back street and back-room abortions before Roe vs. Wade gave women the freedom of choice. Hundreds of thousands of women were badly harmed by untrained people working illegally out of dirty back rooms. Many lost their ability to bear more children and many more died of complications.

As teenage girls in the 1950s, '60s and early '70s, we had little freedom. The number of us who were raped, date-raped, impregnated, and abused physically, emotionally and sexually is astronomical. Among the worst tragedies is that, for the most part, we were led to believe we were responsible for the crimes committed against us.

Amazingly, the majority of us survived our early traumas and lived somewhat healthy, happy lives, proving our immense courage, strength, and perseverance. After all we have been through, these attributes have brought us to new and powerful places in our lives. It is time to open our arms, embrace the freedoms we have achieved in our lifetimes, and then stand up against any and all who threaten those freedoms for our daughters, and granddaughters.

Questions to Ponder

- *What do you remember from your teen years about your lack of freedom?*
- *Did you ever feel as if someone stole your freedom from you?*
- *Do you believe that young women today have more freedom than you had? If so, what kinds of freedoms do you think they have?*

FREEDOM TO BE ME

"Freedom breeds freedom. Nothing else does."

– Anne Roe

During the course of this book, we have focused our attention on the powers of Self-Love, Creativity, Self-Trust, Courage and Ability, Health and Beauty, True Wealth, Our Own Direction, Partnership and Community, Authentic Leadership, and Enlightened Success. Each of these Points of Power alone is potent, but combined, they are the recipes for FREEDOM.

Not merely old ideas of freedom that were the limited gifts of our forefathers, but a new kind of freedom for women—women who have had the courage to walk through the fires of life's lessons. This is the freedom to live the life for which we were born. It is the freedom to express fully and completely who we truly are.

On this journey, we have begun opening some of the doors that have been locked to us for large portions of our lives. The doors may not be open wide, in fact some may only be opened a tiny crack, but the light behind these cracked doors is seeping out around the edges and illuminating pathways in the darkness. Your freedom lies in your commitment to opening the doors even wider. You must be vigilant. Without attention, they will slam shut again very quickly. With attention and focus, you will eventually be able to fling them wide. The light may be blinding.

To step into freedom takes courage. Think of yourself as a prisoner who has been locked in the dark for many years. The bright sunlight and lack of restraints will be difficult adjustments. Freedom requires different skills than prison. With the tools, techniques, games, and disciplines you've learned during this Power Woman course, you are developing new freedom skills.

As prisoners, we learned to survive with obedience, silence, and subservience. Sometimes, we even got a little extra scrap from the jailer by using flattery, subterfuge, and/or prostitution. As free women, we must willingly relinquish the tools of minimal survival, so that we can develop the tools for an expansive, powerful life. This won't be easy. The desire to return to normalcy is strong in all of us. But complacency does not bring freedom.

To be all that you came into this life to be is your heart's deepest desire. Step onto the stage. Use all your talent, your entire beautiful mind, all your intuition, and all your strength. Don't do it for anyone else. Don't do it for your children. Don't do it for your mother. Don't do it even for the women who will follow in your footsteps. Do it for yourself. When you have your freedom it will be easier to help others get theirs.

Recently, my good friend, writer and filmmaker Hope Perello—who is forty-five and taking the first steps on her menopausal journey—said, "We Western women have an amazing amount of freedom now. Society has actually granted us more freedom than we have taken advantage of. We really can have it all, but many women suffer because they don't feel free themselves, because they still follow the roles set out for them. No one today tells us that we can't have anything. Some women are timid to reach for their freedom. It's no longer the laws that stop us. The superficial barriers have broken down, but the real barriers, which are the hardest to break, come from within. We are actually imprisoned by our own lack of imagination.

"And choices. We have so many choices, which means so many wrong choices are possible. When someone is forcing you to do something, you have no choice. You may be oppressed, but it can seem so much easier. If you're no longer oppressed it's scary. It's unpredictable. We see it in abusive marriages. It often seems easier to an abused woman to take the abuse than to leave. It takes great inner strength to become free. It's the inner landscape we have to explore so that we can take on the outer landscape."

Questions to Ponder

- *What kinds of freedom do you most wish to have in your life now?*
- *What can you do today to open a door to your freedom wider?*

LETTING GO IS FREEDOM

Each of us carries around tons of old ideas and antiquated thinking about how things should be done. We learned them from our parents, our school chums, our partners, books, magazines, films, and television. During our lifetimes, we carefully constructed belief systems from all this information, and it has served us up to this point.

But as we move into the second half of life, many of these old constructs have become blocks to our continued progress. It is my hope that in this course you are recognizing and disconnecting from that which no longer works for you. The more we disconnect from the old prohibiting ideas, the more we will begin to understand true freedom.

The chorus in Kris Kristofferson's song, "Me and Bobby Magee"—which Janis Joplin recorded more than thirty years ago—"Freedom's just another word for nothing left to lose" is one of the most profound meditations I have ever known. When we lose everything, we gain the world. When we have lost everything, we have no other choice but to give up control.

And when we give up control, we realize that there, in the midst of nothingness, is Spirit. And in the middle of Spirit is our true self.

It is from this powerful place that we now step. The passage of menopause is our delivery through our own wombs into our new lives. With Divine Spirit as our partner, and nothing left to lose, we are free to be exactly who we were meant to be.

As Power Women, we have the potential to be the most commanding force for good on the planet. We have the Divine Mother on our side. We have our Divine Spirits with us at all times. We have the talent, experience, and love necessary to help the human race survive and thrive in the new era. We simply have to believe that it's so.

Yet none of us can do it alone. Our kind of leadership manifests in partnership, in community, and in cooperation. We only have to have the courage to accept our freedom and take responsibility for what that entails.

GAMES AND EXERCISES

WEEK ELEVEN: THE POWER OF FREEDOM

1. Make a list of five things that you find to frightening to do. Choose one and do it.

2. Go alone to the most beautiful place in nature that you can find in your area. Climb to a high point, open your arms, feel the beauty of the place enveloping you. Sing a song. Feel the freedom.

3. Go through your music collection and choose a favorite oldies CD. Put it on and dance to it. Feel the freedom of dancing alone to your teenage music. Sing along. Don't stop until you can't dance or sing another instant.

4. Telephone someone from out of your past. Preferably someone who has cropped up in your thoughts throughout the course. Just chat.

GAMES AND EXERCISES

SPECIAL TASKS: The next and final step on this journey is the ceremony and celebration to acknowledge the passage into your Power Woman. For that you will need a few things that you can begin preparing now. Make sure to bring these things to use in your ceremony.

They are:
1. Find a beautiful candle and make or decorate a holder for it. (The holder needs to be able to stand on its own.)

2. Write one or two paragraphs describing some of the changes you have experienced through this course.

3. Write a poem about FREEDOM.

4. Choose two or three favorite songs from your teenage years to use during your celebration.

REMEMBER to journal and meditate daily. By this time your journaling and meditations have become an integral and powerful part of your daily life. Don't let them go just because you're coming to the end of this leg of your journey. Keep them as your basic life tools. Using them will help you continue to grow more deeply in tune with your Spirit and more acutely aware of your part in the mysteries of the universe.

The Final Ceremony

"Tomorrow is here at this moment now, with us, among us, in us, but not quite born. Messages are coming to us all the time from tomorrow. It makes embryo noises to us through the most unlikely channels. Tomorrow aches to be born… Love is turning us into the next stage."

– Jean Houston

O ur souls crave celebration. Our hearts become more open when we participate in rituals and ceremonies.

During the past thirty or forty years, our culture has reassessed its participation in ceremony. Many people have turned their backs on ceremonies, including the marriage ceremony, preferring to simply live with a partner without the ritual. Many proponents of partnership without ceremony believe that the sanction of the state is not necessary for their union. Others find traditional religious rites empty and devoid of meaning. But most likely what these opponents of ceremony are rejecting are the trappings, not the substance, of ceremony. It is the inclusion of a higher consciousness, or Divine Spirit, which is the true essence of ceremony. Real ceremony exists, whether or not it is traditional, when Divine Consciousness is invited to be a major participant. This inclusion of the Divine in any ceremony, ritual, or in fact, in any moment in time, transforms the event and the participants.

When we last saw Inanna, she'd just arrived back on Earth as a wild woman seething with newfound power. She is so intense that no one and nothing can stand in her way. She is the all-powerful feminine with the stench of death still clinging to her.

Enheduanna, the Sumerian priestess who wrote about Inanna in 2300 BCE, describes the return of the goddess, and that "she is like a bird who scavenges the land, charges like a raging storm across the Earth, roaring, thundering, rampaging, she moves restlessly carrying her harp of sighs and breathing the music of mourning."

The gods surround her, watching with admiration and terror. Who is this new goddess? Only Ninshubur and her closest women can come near. They know what to do. They know that out of this rawness comes great power, but they also know that this great power must have form and direction.

Inanna must be anointed. Her wounds must be cleansed and the horrible smells of the underworld must be washed away. Then, and only then, will she be able to direct her fierce new power.

The women are called to come around her. They don their priestess robes and perform a holy ceremony of initiation. They sing songs to the goddess to soothe her soul. They pour healing oils on her wounds. They wash away death's hideous stench with sweet smelling rose water. They read to her poems of her greatness. They remind her that she is the "Lady of all Powers in whom light appears." She is the "Radiant one...the guardian of all greatness."

The women dance to the rhythm of their own hearts, until at last Inanna's heart opens and she feels love. In the support of this community of women, she experiences her own aliveness. By the end of the ceremony, Inanna stands in her new power, without rage. She left as a daughter and a wife. Now she is the all-powerful Mother of the World, healed in ceremony by the love of her women. As she rises, all the Gods of Heaven welcome and praise her. Life on Earth is resurrected, for "Inanna's heart is restored...The doorsill of heaven cries 'Hail! Praise to the destroyer endowed with power, to my lady enfolded in beauty. Praise to Inanna.'"

To bring your own wild, raw Spirit into harmony so that you may express all that you have become during your journey through the Eleven Points of Power, you, too, will need to engage in a soothing ceremony of reinstatement.

In ancient times, each of life's thresholds was crossed with the assistance of ceremony. Now, as you come of age in the second half of your life, you will create a ceremony of initiation and transformation to embrace and embody your Power Woman fully and completely. In circle, each new Power Woman is Inanna. Each new Power Woman must be anointed and honored by all the women so that she too can step across the "doorsill of heaven" and claim her power. Those of you who are doing this ceremony alone, be sure to use your imagination to the fullest. Imagine yourselves surrounded by all the great women of the world welcoming you into your power. Embracing you in their sisterhood.

The following is a suggested ceremony. Use it as is, add to it, change it, or invent your very own. What's vital is that you celebrate your passage. You can enact a ceremony alone, but if you are in a circle, you will want to join together for this passage.

TOOLS FOR A SUGGESTED CEREMONY

To perform this ceremony you will need ceremonial tools. The tools are the same for a solo ceremony or a group ceremony. Gather them beforehand.

- *One large candle to stand in the center of the circle or on the altar.*
- *One smudge stick.*
- *A fireplace, barbecue, or large pot in which you can burn things safely.*
- *A basket of dried leaves, dried sticks, or pine needles for starting a fire.*
- *One wine glass for each participant.*
- *Perfumed oil.*
- *Red wine and/or some other red juice—enough for each person to have one glassful.*
- *Fresh fruit for each participant.*
- *A small piece of paper about 3" by 4" for each participant.*
- *A pen or pencil for each participant.*
- *Spirit-centered music.*
- *Copies of the Women's Prayer from page 43 of this book.*

Additionally, each person should bring to the ceremony:

- *Your candle from the "Power of Freedom" chapter's Special Tasks.*
- *The paragraph you wrote describing your changes during the course.*
- *Your Freedom poem.*

THE CEREMONY

To prepare for the ceremony:

- One woman will light the candle in the center of the circle or on the altar.

- Another woman (or this can be shared by everyone taking turns) will light the smudge stick and smudge the room with the sacred smoke to clear out unwanted energy and open the space for ceremony.

- Each woman will place everything she has brought to the ceremony in front of her or within easy reach.

To begin the ceremony:

- Sit in front of the lit candle. In a group it is best to sit in a circle around the candle.

- Close your eyes and begin the Yin-Yang Energy Meditation. (Someone can lead the meditation, or each person can direct herself through the meditation. This should be decided beforehand.)

The Meditation:

- Go into your Sacred Room. Light your White Star and join with your beloved teenage self and your Spirit.

- Descend to your Sacred Cave and experience the Power of the Great Mother's dark violet light energy.

- Ask the Great Mother and your Spirit to help you become aware of whatever you need to release so that you can experience your true Freedom and step fully into your new Power Woman on this day.

- Return to your Sacred Room and begin the downpour of white light.

- Follow the downpour of white light with the up-pour of dark violet light, and let your body begin to move with the rhythm as the energies, the light and the dark, dance and swirl through you. Surrender to the light and allow the old blocks to your true Freedom to fall into the fires of the white light and the dark violet light. And open to experience the birth of your Power Woman.

- When you have completed the meditation, open your eyes and look into the candle.

Continuing the Ceremony:

- One woman will turn on the spirit-centered music softly. (Decide which music and whose task this will be beforehand.)

- Each woman will light her personal candle from the altar candle.

- While focusing on her candle flame, each woman will read out loud her prepared paragraphs of the changes she has experienced during the course.

- Each woman will take a piece of the paper she has brought and write down one thing that she became aware of during the meditation, which she now needs to release in order to achieve true freedom.

- One woman will light the fire in the fireplace or burning pot with the dried leaves, sticks, etc. (Decide on this person beforehand.)

- One by one, each woman will bring her piece of paper to the fire. If she wishes, she may choose to tell the circle what she is releasing. She will then place the paper in the fire. If safe, she can throw more dried leaves onto the fire to symbolize that this is an old part of her that is dead and needs to disappear like the dead leaves. She will stare silently into the fire until her piece of paper is burned completely. The other women in the circle will support her silence.

- When everyone has completed the burning ritual, each woman will take a bite of fruit to replenish her body and spirit symbolizing new life.

- Each woman will then read her Freedom poem while focusing on the flame of her own candle.

- One by one, each woman will stand and step into the center of the circle to be anointed as a Power Woman by the others with perfumed oil, and expressions of love and appreciation and the good the new Power Woman will bring to the world.

- Everyone will read the Women's Prayer together, out loud.

- Pour and drink the wine (or red juice), symbolizing the blood of the great Mother Earth, the mother of us all.

- Turn up the music and dance for as long as you wish.
  Celebrate your freedom.

THE CELEBRATION AND FEAST

After the ceremony indulge in a feast. This should be a potluck where everyone contributes. After feasting, dance and party for the rest of the night.

If you are doing the ceremony on your own, take yourself out for a wonderful meal, or a hike and a picnic in the country. Celebrate your magnificence!!!

GAMES AND EXERCISES

WEEK TWELVE AND BEYOND

1. Start the process again. This course can be done repeatedly. Each time, you will go to a deeper level where you will reveal and own more and more of your powerful potential.

2. Journal and Meditate every day.

3. Pass the word: Women over forty-five are going to transform the world.

4. Imagine your first step as a Power Woman in the world.

5. Take your first step as a Power Woman in the world.

6. Watch without judgment and acknowledge the peace.

7. Stay in the moment. Do something unexpected.

8. Expect Miracles!

9. Honor your spirit, your brilliance, your beauty, and your power for the rest of your life.

10. If you are in a circle, keep your circle going. If you are doing this alone, perhaps you will want to form a circle to do the work again with like-minded others.

ENJOY YOUR POWERFUL LIFE!

Appendix 1

GUIDELINES FOR FORMING A CIRCLE

It's best to hold circle meetings once a week in members' homes or in a location that is comfortable and conducive to creating sacred space and emotional safety. If you do it in your homes, it's best to rotate so that no woman has to carry the burden of preparing for company every week.

A circle of women is not a hierarchy in any way. In a circle, each woman is equal to every other woman. Each woman brings her own unique talents to the circle. Hierarchies are the way men work best. Women work best in communities of equals. Therefore, although one woman may have initiated the circle, she is not the head of the circle, because circles have no heads.

Women should take turns facilitating in whatever way best suits the individual circle. It may work well for your circle if you rotate each week and have one woman lead all the evening's events, or you may wish to share the duties by having a different woman facilitate each part of the meeting.

Circles consist of a group of women who have reached mid-life or beyond. (Mid-life varies from woman to woman, but usually begins somewhere in our forties.) The number of women in a circle may vary, but it's best to keep it between five and eleven (the number of feminine mastery). More than eleven can make it difficult for each person to have time to share at every gathering. Seven is a great number.

As Sherri S. Tepper says, "Against seven no gate may stand."

SUGGESTIONS FOR THE FIRST MEETING

At the first meeting of your circle, after everyone has introduced herself, go around the room taking turns reading the Introduction and the first chapter, "Getting Started." Then look ahead in the book and see how each chapter is laid out. You will notice that the chapters are designed to be studied for one week. Therefore, your circles should meet on a weekly basis, so that you can come back to the circle after the completion of each chapter to share your experiences with the tools, games and exercises, and to prepare for the upcoming week.

There are Eleven Points of Power, so there are eleven chapters to be done for eleven weeks. You will need two extra weeks, one to begin and one for the final week's ceremony and celebration, making it a total of thirteen weeks.

SUGGESTIONS FOR WEEKLY MEETINGS

It is important always to approach your circle as a sacred space. When you first arrive at the location where the circle is being held, try to keep talking to a minimum until after the meditation.

The first order of the evening is the meditation, as soon as everyone has arrived. This brings the whole group into a peaceful, focused state. Have a different person lead the meditation each week. (The meditation is described in Week One. There is an outline of the meditation in Appendix II for easy referral.)

The experience of leading a meditation is very different from being guided through a meditation, so it's important for all members of the circle to experience both leading and being guided. If leading a meditation seems too daunting, you can play a tape recording of yourself reading the meditation directly from the book.

Following the meditation, go around the circle and listen while each person speaks briefly about the experience of her meditation. Talking about our meditative experiences helps integrate our Spirit selves with our personalities. Our goal is to become ever more in tune with our Spirit selves.

Next, structure a short amount of time for reports by all members on their ability or inability to maintain the daily journaling and meditation. For those having trouble, the others may want to gently share how they are able to keep to the routine.

After that, go over the essays in the previous chapter. Talk about parts of the chapter that affected each person and what you gained from it. Perhaps read sections of the chapter out loud. Discuss the "Questions to Ponder."

Next, take a break. Have a cup of tea and some free chatting time. This should last for no more than fifteen minutes, because you want to stay in the flow of the circle. But breathers are necessary for women to get to know each other out of the context of the work.

After the break, form small groups of three or four people to discuss the games and exercises of the previous week's Point of Power. What was it like to do the exercises and games? Which ones did you enjoy doing? Which ones did you find challenging? Express any insights you gained from them. This should last about thirty minutes. Also, it's important to change the make up of the small groups each week, so that the circle remains a circle and doesn't become a collection of small cliques.

To complete the evening, return to the circle. Share anything that you feel needs to be shared. Some weeks there are creative projects such as collages. Bring your completed projects to the circle and exhibit them at this time. Before you leave the circle, say the Women's Prayer (see page 43) together in unison. Then close your eyes for a moment of meditation where you gather into your hearts all the goodness that has come from this meeting of emerging Power Women. A group hug is always wonderful before leaving the circle for the week.

Remember: All members of your circle, like all women on Earth, are sisters. We are here to love and help each other. Call a circle member when you're having a tough time, and be there for your fellow circle members when they need your shoulder to lean on.

Appendix 2

THE YIN–YANG ENERGY MEDITATION—OUTLINE

1. Take three deep breaths to release tension.
2. Harmonize your breathing and all the rhythms of your body with the rhythms of the Earth, and feel yourself being supported by the Great Mother.
3. Focus your attention in your third eye, disconnecting from all your daily cares.
4. Move with your focused attention up into your eighth chakra – six to eight inches above your head. This is your Sacred Room. Spend some time relaxing here in whatever way you choose.
5. Go out the door and walk down a path until you meet your teenage self. (As you progress through the course, the teenage self you encounter will not always be the same age. Be sure to pay attention to which stage of your teenage self you are meeting with today.) Embrace your teenage self. Dance together.
6. Light your White Star.
7. Direct the white liquid light energy to pour down from your Star though your head, upper chest, arms, and hands.
8. Think of the palms of your hands opening and allow the white light to flow out of them.
9. Continue the downpour of pure white light energy through your entire body, down your legs and into your feet.
10. Think of the bottoms of your feet opening and let the light carry the psychic debris that it has picked up along the way out of your body and down into the Earth. Become aware of the subtle changes taking place in your body.

11. Move three feet below your feet and enter your Sacred Cave. Explore your cave. Meet your Power Woman and embrace her.

12. Light your dark violet sun. Direct the dark (almost black) violet light energy to pour up through your feet, legs, body, arms, throat, head, and out the top of your head. Then direct the dark violet energy to wrap around your body like a cloak.

13. Focus on your physical body as the dark violet Yin light moves up, and the white Yang light moves down.

14. Observe the sensations in your body as the Yin and Yang light energies dance and swirl through your body, and flow out and around your body. Float in the light and sink into the light. Wherever you feel any pain or constriction, direct the light into that part of your body, intensify the light, and allow the light to begin healing.

15. Move up into your Sacred Room and direct the downpour of white light to stop.

16. Move down into your Sacred Cave and direct the up-pour of dark violet light to stop.

17. Close the bottoms of your feet, the palms of your hands, and the top of your head.

18. Stand in your power as a lighted being.

19. Send light around the circle clockwise if you are doing this in the circle, or around the world in your private meditation.

20. Take a deep breath. Wiggle your fingers and toes. Plant your feet solidly on the floor. Open your eyes slowly.

21. ENJOY the feeling of well being.

Bibliography

Angelou, Maya. *The Complete Collected Poems of Maya Angelou.* New York: Random House, 1994.

Arrien, Angeles. *The Second Half Of Life.* Audio-Cassette. Boulder, CO: Sounds True, 1998.

Baring, Anne, and Jules Cashford. *The Myth of the Goddess: Evolution of an Image.* London: Viking Arkana, 1991.

Bolen, Jean Shinoda. *The Millionth Circle: How to Change Ourselves and the World.* Berkeley: Conari Press, 1999.

Bonder, Nilton. Translator, Adriana Kac. *The Kabbalah of Money: Insights on Livelihood, Business, and All Forms of Economic Behavior.* Boston & London: Shambhala, 1996.

Borysenko, Joan. *A Woman's Book of Life: The Biology, Psychology, and Spirituality of the Feminine Life Cycle.* New York: Riverhead Books, 1996.

Cameron, Julia. *The Artist's Way: A Spiritual Path to Higher Creativity.* New York: G.P. Putnam's Sons, 1992.

————. *The Vein of Gold: A Journey to Your Creative Heart.* New York: G.P. Putnam's Sons, 1996.

Chopra, Deepak. *Ageless Body, Timeless Mind: The Quantum Alternative to Growing Old.* New York: Harmony Books, 1993.

Christ, Carol P. *Laughter of Aphrodite: Reflections on a Journey to the Goddess.* San Francisco: Harper & Row, 1987.

Eisler, Rianne. *The Chalice and the Blade.* San Francisco: Harper & Row, 1987.

Diamant, Anita. *The Red Tent.* New York: Picador USA, 1997.

Dyer, Wayne. *The Power of Intention: Learning to Co-create Your World Your Way.* Carlsbad, CA: Hay House, Inc., 2004

Hirshfield, Jane, editor. *Women in Praise of the Sacred: 43 Centuries of Spiritual Poetry by Women.* New York: Harper Perennial, 1994.

Irigaray, Luce. *To Be Two.* New York: Routledge, 2001.

MacCulloch, J.A. *The Religion of the Ancient Celts.* London: Studio Editions, 1992.

Markale, Jean. *The Celts: Uncovering the Mythic and Historic Origins of Western Culture.* Rochester, Vermont: Inner Traditions International, 1978.

Muten, Burleigh. *Return of the Great Goddess.* Boston & London: Shambhala, 1994.

Myss, Caroline. *Anatomy of the Spirit: The Seven Stages of Power and Healing.* Harmony Books. New York: Harmony Books, 1996.

Needleman, Jacob. *Money and the Meaning of Life.* New York: Currency/ Doubleday, 1991.

Northrup, Christiane. *The Wisdom of Menopause: Creating Physical and Emotional Health During the Change.* New York: Bantam Books, 2001.

Patai, Raphael. *The Hebrew Goddess.* Detroit: Wayne State University Press, 1990.

Perera, Sylvia Brinton. *Descent to the Goddess: A Way of Initiation for Women.* Toronto: Inner City Books, 1981.

Schofield, Russell Paul, and Carol Ann Schofield. *The Basic Principles of Actualism.* San Diego, California: Actualism Trust, 1971.

Shlain, Leonard. *The Alphabet Versus the Goddess: The Conflict Between Word and Image.* New York: Penguin/Arkana, 1999.

Tacitus, Cornelius, Translator, Michael Grant. *Tacitus: The Annals of Imperial Rome.* Baltimore, Maryland: Penguin Books, 1962.

Walker, Barbara G. *The Woman's Encyclopedia of Myths and Secrets.* San Francisco: Harper & Row, 1983.

Wilder, Barbara. *Money is Love: Reconnecting to the Sacred Origins of Money.* Boulder, Colorado: Wild Ox Press, 1999.

Williamson, Marianne. *A Woman's Worth.* New York: Ballantine, 1994.

Woolf, Virginia. *A Room of One's Own.* New York: First Harvest/HGJ, Harcourt Brace Jovanovich, 1989.

TO ORDER BOOKS OR
TO SCHEDULE BARBARA WILDER TO SPEAK
OR LEAD WORKSHOPS AND RETREATS

based on

EMBRACING YOUR POWER WOMAN

and/or

MONEY IS LOVE

Contact:

Wild Ox Press
P.O. Box 3304
Boulder, CO 80307-3304
Email: info@barbarawilder.com

And please visit the Website at www.BarbaraWilder.com

ABOUT THE AUTHOR

Barbara Wilder is an internationally acclaimed author, teacher, and healer. A former actress, screenwriter, and film production executive, Wilder studied light-energy healing and growth techniques in The School of Actualism, a Hermetic Mystery school based on Agni Yoga & the works of Alice Bailey & Rudolf Steiner. She currently lives in Boulder, Colorado, where she writes, teaches, and maintains her practice as an intuitive counselor and light-energy transformational healer, and plays ball with her beloved dog, Gage.

For more information on Barbara and her work, please visit her website www.BarbaraWilder.com